Equal Voice Voting
Making Our Votes Count in the Electoral College

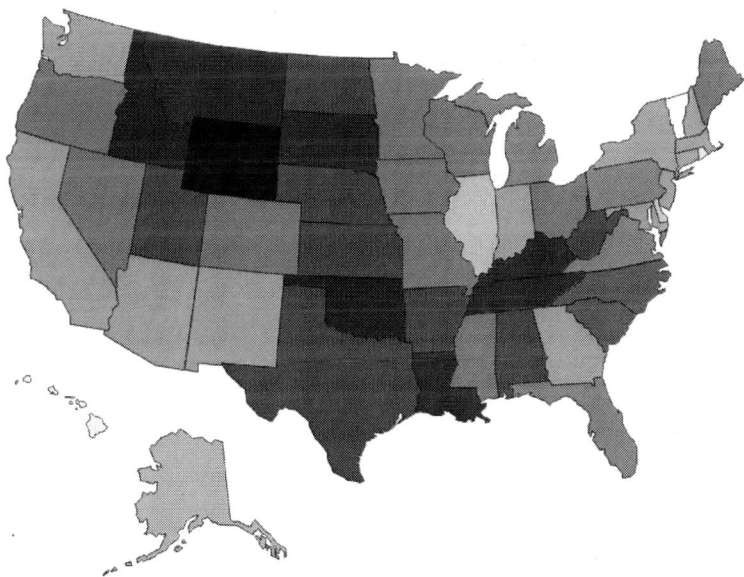

By
Jerry Spriggs

Becky
Thanks for
your support!
Keep every
voter engaged!

Equal Voice Voting

Acknowledgements

This book has come to fruition through the sage advice and kind support from many people. It would not have happened without the ready reference and data gleaned from Dave Leip's Atlas of Presidential Elections data (http://uselectionatlas.org). My wife, Jane, has patiently listened to my wrestling with the thoughts and "what-if" speculations as I slowly derived a better solution with Equal Voice Voting. She has been a great sounding board, always providing a voice of reason to stave off what would have been a rather awkward presentation. Friends have weighed in with either their supporting voice or gentle nudges to make the presentation stronger, or both. My editor, Tricia Plourd, has been essential in correcting the grammar and language used and has been particularly supportive in bringing this work to fruition. To all of these I humbly express my gratitude. Their efforts and energy has truly made all of this fun – an essential element of life!

Cover Art: The map of the United States is shaded in relation to the Equal Vote Voting results for 2012, showing representation for the Democratic and Republican representation in each state.

Table of Contents

Table of Figures

List of Tables

INTRODUCTION

The state of this nation's Electoral College is a mess! Because of the rules we are forced to follow every time we try to elect a president, a large share of the population's votes are not counted and many other could-be voters simply don't bother to vote. It's time to change the rules!

When I say that many votes are not counted, I'm not referring to some kind of mismanaged process wherein votes get lost or are purged from the system. Rather, I'm referring to the fact that our Electoral College system ignores a large portion of votes. Those voices disappear!

The 2012 presidential election had 129,132,140 votes cast. Of those, 56,431,932 votes (43.7%) were NOT represented in the Electoral College when it came time to tally the final results. Those 53 plus million voters could just as easily have stayed home, not wasted their time, done something else a little more productive that day.

48 states and one district (Washington D.C.) have a winner-takes-all rule when it comes for them to cast their electoral votes. That means that if you live in a state wherein the majority of voters vote for another candidate than you do, your vote is not represented in the Electoral College. Those other two states (Maine and Nebraska – see Winner Takes All, page 25) might as well use the winner-takes-all approach, given the results they've realized since instituting their new rules because they have only cast their respective electoral votes for one candidate in the presidential elections. Again, votes are discarded in the sense they have no impact on the Electoral College.

Let me show you what I mean with a simple table showing the votes that disappeared in 2012 (Leip, 2012).

Table 1: Votes Not Represented in 2012

States	Votes Not Counted	% of Votes Not Counted	States	Votes Not Counted	% of Votes Not Counted
AL	818,413	39.45%	MT	216,120	44.65%
AK	135,819	45.20%	NE	319,315	40.20%
AZ	1,072,905	46.52%	NV	483,545	47.64%
AR	421,724	39.43%	NH	341,411	48.02%
CA	5,184,262	39.76%	NJ	1,523,101	41.78%
CO	1,246,219	48.51%	NM	368,422	47.01%
CT	653,884	41.94%	NY	2,590,054	36.68%
DE	171,306	41.39%	NC	2,234,977	49.61%
DC	26,694	9.09%	ND	134,612	41.68%
FL	4,252,406	50.09%	OH	2,753,201	49.33%
GA	1,821,362	46.70%	OK	443,547	33.23%
HI	128,039	29.45%	OR	818,782	45.76%
ID	235,831	35.91%	PA	2,763,619	48.03%
IL	2,224,662	42.42%	RI	166,372	37.30%
IN	1,203,991	45.87%	SC	892,473	45.44%
IA	759,636	48.01%	SD	153,205	42.11%
KS	467,337	40.29%	TN	996,247	40.52%
KY	710,022	39.51%	TX	3,424,008	42.83%
LA	841,803	42.22%	UT	279,215	27.38%
ME	311,874	43.73%	VT	100,051	33.43%
MD	1,029,483	38.03%	VA	1,882,669	48.84%
MA	1,246,477	39.35%	WA	1,385,710	44.12%
MI	2,175,681	45.90%	WV	252,783	37.70%
MN	1,390,394	47.35%	WI	1,450,449	47.22%
MS	574,838	44.71%	WY	78,099	31.36%
MO	1,274,883	46.24%			
Total Votes = 56,431,932 = 43.7% of Votes Cast					

These are votes cast for a candidate that did not win the majority popular vote within the state or district in which they were cast. Because of our current rules, these votes have no representation in the Electoral College. The winner-takes-all mentality must be changed!

Let's do a quick review of the 2012 presidential election. Obama won the popular vote over Romney with a 3.84% margin. That's fairly close. He won the Electoral College vote over Romney by a 38.3% margin. That's a significant margin. However, considering that only 56.3% of the votes cast had representation in the Electoral College, Obama won the election with only 36.9% of these votes (47,616,118 votes). Romney captured 19.43% of the votes (25,184,090 votes) represented in the Electoral College.

There were 207,643,594 eligible voters in 2012. Only 129,132,140 (62.2%) voted. Since only 62.2% of eligible voters voted in this election, Obama won the election with only 22.9% of the eligible voters selecting him and being represented in the Electoral College. It means even fewer eligible voters (12.08%) chose Romney and were represented in the Electoral College.

- Eligible Voters in 2012 = 207,643,594

- Popular Votes = 129,132,140 (62.2% of Eligible Voters)

- Votes Represented in Electoral College = 72,700,208

- Votes for Obama Represented in Electoral College = 47,616,118 Votes (65.5%)

- Votes for Romney Represented in Electoral College = 25,084,090 Votes (34.5%)

- Eligible Voters Represented in Electoral College

    ✓ Obama = 22.9%
    ✓ Romney = 12.08%

Our current system is not a model for a true democracy.

Do **you** care? I doubt many readers of this book could be considered apathetic about their vote or their voting rights. That's an assumption on my part, but when I mentioned that many voters don't bother to vote, it's not simply apathy that's my central concern. I believe that many have already broken the code of the Electoral College rules and realized that their vote won't make a difference!

If you realize that you're among the minority voters within your state, you might question why you should bother to cast your vote? You probably already realize yours is a lost cause. Or, if you are a voter in a state that is predominantly in your favor, you may not be encouraged to vote because, after all, many of your friends and neighbors will vote as you would and get your candidate elected anyway. Your vote really isn't needed.

The low voter turn-out this nation experiences during presidential elections is not because our nation has citizens who are lazy or apathetic or unpatriotic. It's largely because those voters realize that their vote simply won't matter!

We must have better voting rules so our nation's citizens can have their voices (votes) heard (represented). All of us need an equal voice when we vote for our next president.

There is no immediate need to abolish the Electoral College, which requires a constitutional amendment. We simply have to modify the system so it better reflects our intention to give full measure to our voting citizenry.

Before you jump to the conclusion that I have a solution of how votes should be physically counted, correcting the errors that distract from our presidential elections, be aware that I am not addressing the mechanics of vote capture. Those problems persist and a viable solution still needs further attention. A quick and deliberate remedy to ensure every vote is accurately counted remains, as of this writing, an unanswered challenge.

The Electoral College is a process established by our Founding Fathers as a compromise between electing the president by our nation's popular vote or by the members of Congress. The process is noted in Article II of the United States constitution. When you consider that voting is a basic right and a basic tenent of our democratic system, it's obvious we need to consider why the present system fails us and what we can do about it.

It was the 2000 presidential election that first caught my eye, alerting in me a sense of something being fundamentally wrong about how our Electoral College system fails to represent so many voters. I remember watching the red and blue states being displayed on our television news and news print showing that an imbalance exists in our voting process. Something was, and still is, amiss!

The 2000 presidential election caught our attention because the actual voting process was questioned, tested, and failed. A major concern was in the physical counting of the votes. Chads became a household word and voters' intent took center stage yet failed to register – failed to be counted in any coherent, sensible way. It must have seemed ludicrous for other nations, democratic or not, to watch us while we maneuvered around this national tragedy. Our presidential voting process is hardly one to be replicated by other nations.

Another concern surfaces in the midst of this process. The news media plays into the hand of an anti-democratic process as they capture the news. Voters are interviewed as they exit the polls and trends are quickly reported. The voting on the East coast prevails and voters on the West coast become reluctant to cast their vote (their voice) as the candidates are declared to be projected winners/losers early in the game before all polls are closed. Our cherished democracy suffers.

Why Read This Book?

This book presents an improvement of the Electoral College method which I refer to as the Equal Voice (EV) election method. Succinctly, EV combines the power of the popular vote while retaining an equal representation of every state in the country. The following is a topical list of what this book presents:

- **Our Present Electoral College System** – It's good to first understand how our current Electoral College system works. How did it become our shared method for selecting a president? There is a discussion of the reasoning for why we have such a system and the mechanics of how the present system functions. Some concerns over the present Electoral College system are also presented.

- **Electoral College Results** –A description is provided of how electoral votes are currently allocated for each state. That is followed by a comparison of the popular voting with the electoral vote allocation for each state. The 2012 presidential election is presented, in bar graph format, showing how the popular vote compares with the current Electoral College results. The comparison points to how poorly the two correlate and, it is suggested, that this failing becomes a cause for the existing voting apathy among our citizenry.

- **Popular Vote Representation** – The popular vote, alone, fails to represent this country because of the wide variances that exist in the states' population densities. Alaska, our largest state, is very sparsely populated while New Jersey and the Washington D.C. area are heavily populated. A simple popular vote would heavily favor the smaller (more populous) areas and effectively ignore the concerns/issues of our larger states, creating further imbalance in our representative government. How our nation's population is unevenly spread across our 50 states is illustrated. The section also points out how a simple popular vote strategy would still do our citizenry a voting disservice thereby increasing voter apathy.

- **Congressional Districts** – The focus here is on congressional districts and how splitting a state's vote along these lines runs the risk of manipulation and fraudulent control. Gerrymandering is discussed along with an example of a district that has been obviously manipulated to circumvent true representation.

- **Equal Voice Voting Method** – The Equal Voice (EV) voting method is described. Its simple formula and process demonstrates how every vote and voice makes a difference with fair representation. The 2012 presidential election is presented again showing how the EV method would modify the disparities experienced in that election.

- **Media Coverage** – A discussion is provided showing how our news media affects the voting results and voting apathy simply by reporting the predictability of the voting results well ahead of many voters having a chance to cast their ballot. The section presents a plausible reporting timeline for reporting the election results if the nation used the EV voting method.

- **Equal Voice Voting Advantages** – A summary is presented pointing out the advantages that can be realized if the nation modifies the Electoral College and instead uses the Equal Voice voting method.

- **Let's Talk** – You really can make a difference in our presidential elections. You are encouraged to keep the discussion going. Links to find your senators and representative are provided.

- **Appendices** – Presidential elections from 1980 through 2012 (nine in all) are shown in the same table and graphic formats used in the body of this book. It shows the results of past elections along with "what if" scenarios had the EV election method been used. Also, more depictions of gerrymandering are also provided.

Test of Fairness

The presidential elections have always been intriguing to me. However, while watching the recent elections, it has become obvious to me that fairness is not a high standard; or at least not a standard that met my expectation of fair voting practices within our democracy.

Board games have intrigued me since my youth and have become a bit of a hobby for me. I have constructed a number of them and have entertained friends and family with these creations. A key factor in a successful game is how fair it is. Does everyone playing have an equal chance at competing and winning? It's easy to construct rules that will make a game *function*, but it is quite another challenge to ensure that everyone playing gets an equal turn at play and can participate on a level playing field.

Who wins and who loses the elections was not the test of fairness I sought to create a change in the Electoral College. Respect for every party is vital! The test of success for such a method rests on three things:

- **All voting voices must be heard** – So much of the country's citizenry suffer voter apathy because they live in states wherein their respective vote seems to mean little or nothing. This is an injustice that must be rectified if we wish to call ourselves a democracy.

- **The voting mechanism must be simple** – A voting method must be easily understood, easily instituted, and must deliver obvious results. Clarity is essential.

- **No constitutional amendment is needed** – Each state, individually, must be able to adopt a voting method without having to be in concert with a national movement and without requiring a constitutional amendment.

As you read this book, you'll probably become quickly aware of three things:

First, I've been accused of being a bit of a geek in that I have included lots of tables and graphs and such. You don't have to study each of these! As a convenience to some readers, I've placed most of the graphs and tables in the Appendices so you can focus on the most recent election (2012) to appreciate the essence of what's being presented.

Second, this is not a novel that can be considered a page turner. There is no plot line, no character development, no real suspense to lure you ever forward. Rather, it's a book of facts and figures. I'll do my best to guide you through the topics and will show you why I think we should modify the Electoral College and what results we can expect if Equal Voice voting is used. So, you'll find this is rather like a reference book. You may find yourself flipping back-and-forth as you compare years and state results. You may be surprised by what you find. I think it's rather fun, but that refers back to my first point – I can be a bit geeky.

Third, the formula for Equal Voice (EV) voting is new, but the remaining data is public record. I've relied heavily on data that can be easily viewed via the Internet, and I've referred to those sources when I have. I encourage you to visit these same Web sites and do some searching of your own. I have found that voting via our Electoral College is a topic that has interested many. That is encouraging and, hopefully, you'll be a part of the ongoing discussions to help fix the situation.

Equal Voice Voting

OUR PRESENT ELECTORAL COLLEGE SYSTEM

Our present Electoral College system is, well, rather complex and sometimes messy. Let's first look at what our Constitution says, look at some of its history, and finally what it all means for us today.

Constitution

The following is from our U.S. Constitution. The portion in parenthesis is now superseded by the 12ᵗʰ Amendment, which is quoted afterwards.

The executive Power shall be vested in a President of the United States of America. He shall hold his Office during the Term of four Years, and, together with the Vice-President chosen for the same Term, be elected, as follows:

Each State shall appoint, in such Manner as the Legislature thereof may direct, a Number of Electors, equal to the whole Number of Senators and Representatives to which the State may be entitled in the Congress: but no Senator or Representative, or Person holding an Office of Trust or Profit under the United States, shall be appointed an Elector.

(The Electors shall meet in their respective States, and vote by Ballot for two persons, of whom one at least shall not lie an Inhabitant of the same State with themselves. And they shall make a List of all the Persons voted for, and of the Number of Votes for each; which List they shall sign and certify, and transmit sealed to the Seat of the Government of the United States, directed to the President of the Senate. The President of the Senate shall, in the Presence of the Senate and House of Representatives, open all the Certificates, and the Votes shall then be

counted. *The Person having the greatest Number of Votes
shall be the President, if such Number be a Majority of the
whole Number of Electors appointed; and if there be more
than one who have such Majority, and have an equal
Number of Votes, then the House of Representatives shall
immediately chuse by Ballot one of them for President;
and if no Person have a Majority, then from the five
highest on the List the said House shall in like Manner
chuse the President. But in chusing the President, the
Votes shall be taken by States, the Representation from
each State having one Vote; a quorum for this Purpose
shall consist of a Member or Members from two-thirds of
the States, and a Majority of all the States shall be
necessary to a Choice. In every Case, after the Choice of
the President, the Person having the greatest Number of
Votes of the Electors shall be the Vice President. But if
there should remain two or more who have equal Votes,
the Senate shall chuse from them by Ballot the Vice-
President.)*

12th Amendment

As noted above, the 12th Amendment supersedes the last
portion quoted in the Constitution.

*The Electors shall meet in their respective states, and vote
by ballot for President and Vice-President, one of whom,
at least, shall not be an inhabitant of the same state with
themselves; they shall name in their ballots the person
voted for as President, and in distinct ballots the person
voted for as Vice-President, and they shall make distinct
lists of all persons voted for as President, and of all
persons voted for as Vice-President and of the number of
votes for each, which lists they shall sign and certify, and
transmit sealed to the seat of the government of the
United States, directed to the President of the Senate. The
President of the Senate shall, in the presence of the Senate*

*and House of Representatives, open all the certificates
and the votes shall then be counted;*

*The person having the greatest Number of votes for
President, shall be the President, if such number be a
majority of the whole number of Electors appointed; and
if no person have such majority, then from the persons
having the highest numbers not exceeding three on the list
of those voted for as President, the House of
Representatives shall choose immediately, by ballot, the
President. But in choosing the President, the votes shall be
taken by states, the representation from each state having
one vote; a quorum for this purpose shall consist of a
member or members from two-thirds of the states, and a
majority of all the states shall be necessary to a choice.
And if the House of Representatives shall not choose a
President whenever the right of choice shall devolve upon
them, before the fourth day of March next following, then
the Vice-President shall act as President, as in the case of
the death or other constitutional disability of the
President.*

*The person having the greatest number of votes as Vice-
President, shall be the Vice-President, if such number be a
majority of the whole number of Electors appointed, and
if no person have a majority, then from the two highest
numbers on the list, the Senate shall choose the Vice-
President; a quorum for the purpose shall consist of two-
thirds of the whole number of Senators, and a majority of
the whole number shall be necessary to a choice. But no
person constitutionally ineligible to the office of President
shall be eligible to that of Vice-President of the United
States.*

If you find that this sounds a bit confusing, you're not alone. How we select our president and vice president has been anything except clear. It's been downright messy! Here's some of the history our nation has endured.

Electoral College History

We must first realize that we started out small. There were 13 colonies coming together under one flag, which later became the first 13 states. They were grouped together in the Eastern portion of the country and had only around four million people.

It's worth noting that information traveled rather slowly, by today's standards, and that many thought most people were not schooled or aware enough to cast a sensible vote. Some believed only white males who owned land should be able to vote, for example. Some didn't like the idea of political parties either. Some could say that things really haven't changed much in these regards as differing opinions seem to be everywhere.

Trust was not then nor is it now a thread of honor anyone seems to cling to when considering the powers that govern this country. There were a lot of arguments about how the process should be established and, in the beginning years, some rather ugly experiments were tried.

Remember, we're selecting leaders of significant power and, as such, their selection should be a sober and intelligent undertaking. Power struggles seldom (ever?) are neat and tidy. Conflict arises, naturally, but one thing must be remembered: our system of government works. It may not be tidy and it may not satisfy everyone. It's a government of the people, by the people, and for the people. Still, we need to modify the Electoral College so the presidential election is exactly that.

Our Electoral College history includes a lot of attempts at making it a process that could give everyone a fair representation. There have been a lot of attempts and a lot of failures. Here is a synopsis of what we have endured in the past:

1. Let's make Congress select the president! This seemed like a good idea, on the one hand, because Congress included the people who had to work most directly with the president. It would be kind of like selecting your own boss. Then it was realized that it would only encourage envy and revenge and, (horrors!) divisiveness among Congress! Of course it would, since it takes very little to accomplish that kind of problem.

2. Let someone else do it! The idea here was to let each state congress make the selection. Again, the idea of corruption raised its head and cooler heads thought better of it.

Notice that both of these ideas were for those who govern select the nation's leader. It wasn't until later that the idea of letting the citizens make the selection was offered.

3. Finally, our Founding Fathers decided to create a group (college) of Electors who would be knowledgeable about the issues of the day and the merits of the emerging and existing leaders. It was decided that each state would have a number of Electors according the number of people in each state plus two, to represent the number of each state's senators. Thus, they wisely decided to create a system that could respond to the popular sentiment as well as acknowledge the concerns that arise due to geographic representation.

That principle still holds today, so we have a College of Electors who mostly vote as the state population does. 435 Representatives plus 100 Senators = 535 Electors. They also added three Electors to represent Washington, D.C., which gives us the current number of 538 Electors (Electoral Votes) for our presidential elections. This last adjustment was established by the 23rd Constitutional Amendment.

Did you notice that I said, "...mostly vote as the population does?" That's because there have been times when the Electors did NOT vote as the popular vote prescribed. That's happened four times in the past, but has not emerged to be neither a consistent nor seemingly a corrupt system enough to be tossed aside.

One of the interesting things about this design was how the vice president was elected. Remember, there were no political parties when all of this began! So the candidate who won the most electoral votes became the President. The candidate with the second most electoral votes became the vice president.

Stop! Just for a moment, think of what that would mean in today's world. Can you imagine having President Obama and Vice President Romney? How about Obama and Vice President McCain? Or Bush and Kerry? Or Bush and Gore?

Ties were another interesting bit of vote management. If candidates were locked in a tie, the House of Representatives would then make the selection. The Senate would be called upon (it never was) to make the decision if it was still a tie.

Still, the introduction of political parties forced different rule changes for the presidential elections. The big rule changes occurred because of the problem of voting ties raising its head. Oh, and did you know that one of the first political parties was named the Democratic-Republican party? History – it's interesting stuff!

Anyway, I digress. Thomas Jefferson and Aaron Burr, in 1804, were tied (remember, all candidates were still running individually, not as a President/Vice-President combined ticket). So, the House of Representatives went to work to break the tie. Again and again and again! 36 tie votes were cast (along with a lot of back-room negotiations, I'll bet), until Jefferson won the vote. Whew!

It was obvious that this arrangement couldn't persist! Something had to be done! So, Congress went to work and created the 12th Amendment of the Constitution. So, if you think the current Electoral College system is a bit non-representative of the popular sentiment, and that it is a bit awkward (read messy), you're not alone. I agree with you and am recommending another change to it that will not force yet another Constitutional Amendment.

Here are some interesting facts about our current Electoral College:

1. The presidential election is held every four years on the Tuesday after the first Monday in November.

2. All states, except Maine and Nebraska, have a winner-takes-all system that awards all electors to the winning presidential candidate. Maine and Nebraska have a different system, which is explained later in this book (see Winner Takes All, page 25).

3. A meeting of the state electors takes place on the first Monday after the second Wednesday in December after the presidential election. That's when they cast their votes. As mentioned earlier, these electors typically vote according to the popular vote within their state. That means all state electoral votes are cast for whichever candidate won the state's popular vote.

4. A joint session of Congress (House of Representatives and the Senate) meets on the 6th of January in the year following the meeting of the electors. Of course, this date gets shifted if January 6 lands on a weekend. Each state's electoral votes are counted and the winning ticket (president and vice president) are officially declared.

5. The president-elect is sworn in as President of the United States two weeks later on January 20th.

Something Seems Wrong

The most extreme comparison in the years noted in this writing came in 1984. As shown by the map below, only Minnesota (shown in white) and the District of Columbia gave their combined 13 electoral votes to the Democratic Party, while every other state gave their combined 525 electoral votes to the Republican Party (shown in black). Yet, the Democratic Party received 41% of the popular vote.

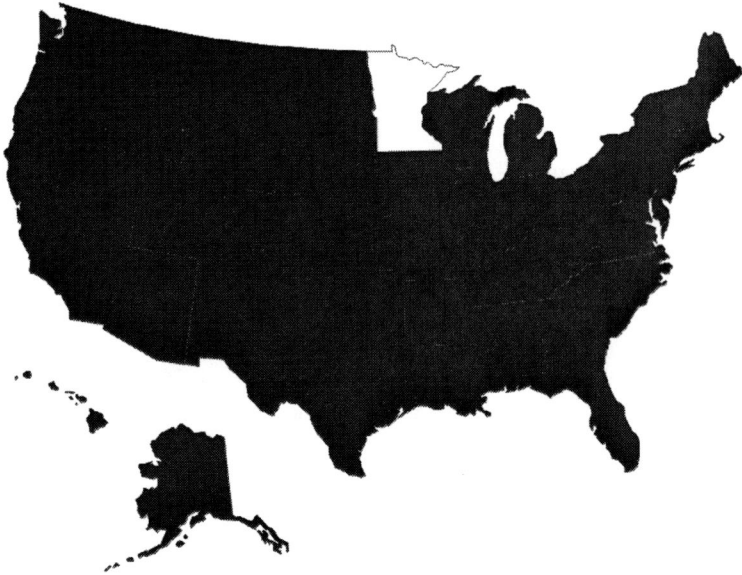

Figure 1: 1984 Electoral Vote Map

If you voted Democratic in this election, you may have resented how the popular vote was ignored or manipulated. If you voted Republican, it may be surprising to see that the Electoral College voting even surpassed the Republican expectation.

This concern for rural representation was also apparent in the highly contentious 2000 election. The map below shows the Electoral College voting results throughout the nation (shown below). 2,432,456 square miles (76% of the nation) are represented in black (Republican) and 575,184 square miles (24% of the nation) are represented in white (Democrat). Still, the popular vote was actually the opposite of this depiction. Republicans lost the popular vote by 216,000 votes.

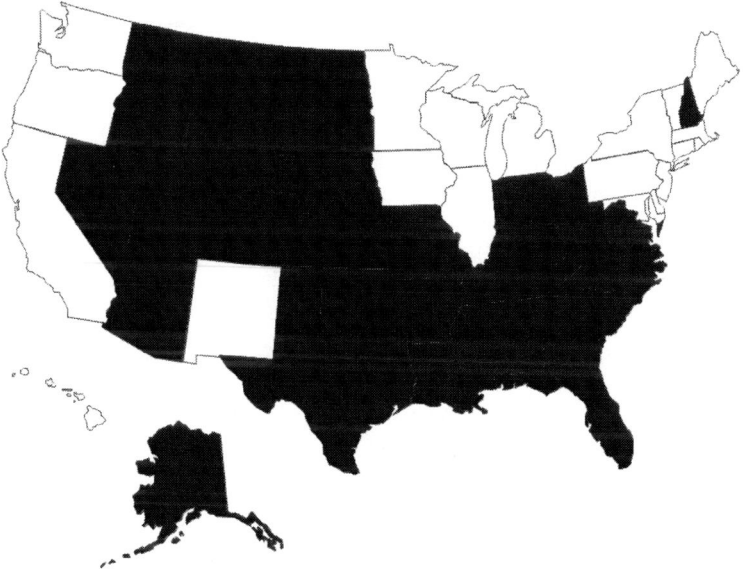

Figure 2: 2000 Electoral Vote Map

A tremendous amount of time, money and energy are spent during every presidential campaign to address the issues, values and beliefs of the voting populace. Yet, as noted in these two examples, our current Electoral College method largely ignores (fails to represent) much of the sentiment of the nation's voters.

Rural America represents those who support our agriculture, mining, lumber, transportation, and fishing industries, to name a few. These types of industries serve the more heavily populated regions within America and the rest of the world. If they are represented simply by a national majority rule, these people and regions do not have an equal voice, as compared to their metropolitan counterparts; yet, they form a critical link to our survival and to our ability to form a positive future for this nation.

For example, imagine a voter resides in a large metropolitan area. This voter's concerns may easily ignore laws that impact farming practices. After all, his/her interactions with the nation's agriculture are minimal, if experienced at all. Still, this voter is directly affected by the price and selection of food, or the availability of cotton or wool clothing. This same voter probably lives in a wood structure and enjoys furniture made of wood. Will he/she be sensitive to the timber industry, both in terms of its sustainable practice and the costs he/she will experience? The same voter probably enjoys the benefits of this nation's mining in that steel is used for his/her car, coal may generate his/her electricity, and precious metals are used in his/her watch or computer or television (to name a few).

Will this voter be aware of the issues they involve if a given candidate fails to address them? Will the voter be aware of what affects our fishing industry if the candidates ignore the rural voter in order to capture the more populous centers of our society?

Such resources are managed by a select few but they serve everyone. These few are tasked with making a living by serving the needs of our general populace for today's needs, as well as attending to the sustainable environmental concerns for generations to come. These few stewards of our land and resources need to have equal representation.

In like manner, those living in rural America may not be sensitive to what is of concern in our cities. Issues surrounding transportation, manufacturing, police, and other concerns may not have the central priority that people living in our population centers may have.

All **geographic regions** are an integral part of our nation's culture. Their geographic representation needs to be acknowledged and fair. The **popular vote** should also be a driving force that is central to selecting our president. This book proposes that the Equal Voice voting method **incorporates both of these two concerns into an easy-to-use and accurate vote counting method.**

ELECTORAL COLLEGE RESULTS

Our Founding Fathers were wise in forming the Electoral College in that it gave voice to the geographic representation of our nation's election process as well as to the popular vote. Also, the Electoral College provides a mechanism to gather the millions of votes across our nation and reduce them to a more manageable – and more meaningful number. There is much that makes sense in our present system, and much that doesn't. Let's look at some of the deficiencies.

Winner Takes All

48 of the 50 states award their electoral votes in a winner-takes-all approach. That means that whichever candidate wins the popular vote in their state, that candidate is awarded all of the electoral votes for that state. It should be noted that a state has a number of electoral votes in proportion to its population. Thus, a state like Alaska only has three electoral votes while California has 55.

For example, if California's popular vote is mostly Democratic, regardless of how close the voting may be, all 55 electoral votes will be awarded to the Democratic candidate. The voting voice of the opposing party is not represented by the Electoral College in that state.

Obama won all of California's 55 electoral votes in 2012 because the popular vote in that state for him was 7,854,285. Romney gained no electoral votes in California that year, though 4,839,958 votes were cast for him.

Similarly, McCain gained 15 electoral votes from Georgia in 2008. The popular vote for him in that state was 2,048,759, as compared to 1,844,123 for Obama. The votes cast for the losing candidate in each of these states did not gain any representation during those two elections!

Voter apathy prevails! If you are a voter in a state that commonly votes for a different candidate than you do, you may be inclined to not vote. On the other hand, if you are a voter in a state that strongly votes for a candidate you like, you may be tempted to disregard your voting privileges because *others will vote like you do!*

Maine and Nebraska are an exception to the rest of the nation in that each gives two electoral votes to the candidate that wins the popular state vote. They then also cast an electoral vote for the winner of each congressional district. Thus, Maine has four electoral votes and Nebraska casts five electoral votes.

While this seemingly gives representation to a state's geography (one of the concerns put forth by this book) the geographic regions of Maine and Nebraska are large and still give more weight to the more populous areas. For example, Maine has two congressional districts representing 14 counties. Nebraska has three congressional districts representing 94 counties. These two states have never split their Electoral College votes since they've begun using this approach.

Again, it would be easy for any voter to assume they are in the minority in any such region and be disinclined to cast their vote as theirs seemingly wouldn't make a difference. **Voter apathy, if corrected, could significantly change the final presidential election results.**

Election Variances

An evaluation of previous elections shows that the present system does not really represent our voters very well, and actually entices some voters to not vote at all. We've already seen how, geographically, the 1984 and 2000 elections were not representative of our nation. The following graph shows that the 2012 popular vote does not match well with the Electoral College results.

Look at the solid bars in the graph below and notice how they vary from each other. The gray bar represents the percentage of the popular vote won by the Obama and the black bar shows how much of the popular vote was won by Romney.

Notice how these solid bars (the popular votes) vary from each other (variance). The popular vote variance is close, showing only a 3.8% separation. This means the voters were rather equally divided in their voting.

In like manner, look at the striped bars. These represent the number of electoral votes a candidate received. The Democrat candidates are represented by the gray striped bars and the Republican candidates are represented by the black striped bars. Notice how much these bars vary from each other. This variance is 23.4%!

The Appendix shows all of the presidential elections from 1980 through 2012. In elections that had third party contenders, those candidates gathered as much as 19% of the popular vote (1992) yet were never represented in the Electoral College in any of the four elections they were counted in the examples shown in the Appendix (1980, 1992, 1996, and 2000).

Popular Vote Versus Electoral College Results

Notice how the popular votes for each candidate compare with the percentage of Electoral Votes.

2012 variances between the Democratic and Republican parties:

Popular Vote (solid bars) = 3.8%
Electoral Vote (striped bars) = 23.4%

2012

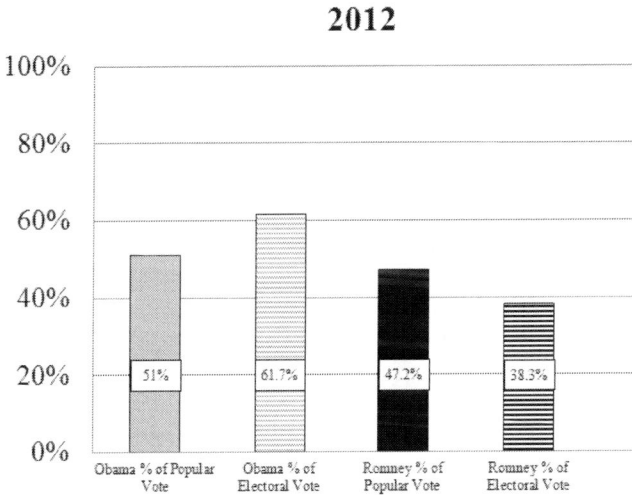

Figure 3: 2012 Vote Comparison Graph

It is interesting to note that in 1984 the popular vote varied by only 18.2% between the Democratic and Republican parties (see Appendix). However, the electoral vote varied as much as 95.2% between those same parties. This is a clear indicator that the present Electoral College system is not reflective of the popular vote.

This comparison shows that when the final tally of votes is made in the Electoral College, a large segment of voters are not represented at all or not represented well. Suppose you are a registered Democrat and plan to vote for the Democratic candidate in the upcoming election. Suppose, however, that you live in a state that usually votes Republican. While you want to be a good citizen and vote, you know that your vote will not have any effect because so many others will vote the opposite of what you will. Knowing this, do you still vote? Will you be disappointed or surprised when your candidate fails in your state? This example can easily be reversed, and be just as unfair, with the example voter being a registered Republican voting in a state that usually votes Democratic.

Voter turn-out, meaning the number of registered voters that actually vote in a presidential election, is typically low nationally. In 2012, the number of eligible voters who voted was around 62%! This is a shame but it is also understandable, given that many voters believe their vote will have little or no consequence.

We currently have a system that effectively disenfranchises and creates apathy among large segments of our voting citizenry on a regular and consistent basis.

POPULAR VOTE REPRESENTATION

One idea to replace the Electoral College that has been put forth is to simply count the popular vote, regardless of geography, to determine the winner. A rather popular bill is currently wending its way through state legislatures called *The National Popular Vote Bill.*

The idea behind The National Popular Vote Bill is that a state makes an agreement to cast all of its electoral votes for whichever candidate wins the national popular vote. It's a simple approach and one that can be lauded for its clever modification to reflect the popular intent of the nation while not incurring the effort needed to modify the U.S. Constitution.

The results at first glance appear to be good because you derive the same result as the national popular vote. However, the citizens within a given state who cast their popular votes for the losing candidates also see all of their electoral votes slipped into another candidate's pocket. Also, the prime attention of any candidate will be focused on the most populous areas (cities, for example). Rural areas with different values, different issues, and different perspectives will see their representation slip away.

One of the intents of our current Electoral College process was to retain representation of our nation's geographic regions on a state level while also attending to the popular vote. It was originally thought that the Electoral College would incorporate both the metropolitan and the rural concerns, simply because more people lived in rural areas as compared to cities.

Geographic Look at the Population

The map below shows how states vary in their population densities. The black and gray filled states are the most densely populated states. As you can see, the population is not evenly spread among states. Consequently, a candidate's attention (and concern) would be for those areas which are more populated.

The nine black states equal ½ of our nation's population!

The 16 gray states equal 1/3rd of our nation's population!

The 25 white states equal only 1/6th of our nation's population! It is quite evident that *The National Popular Vote Bill* approach will largely neglect this large area of our country.

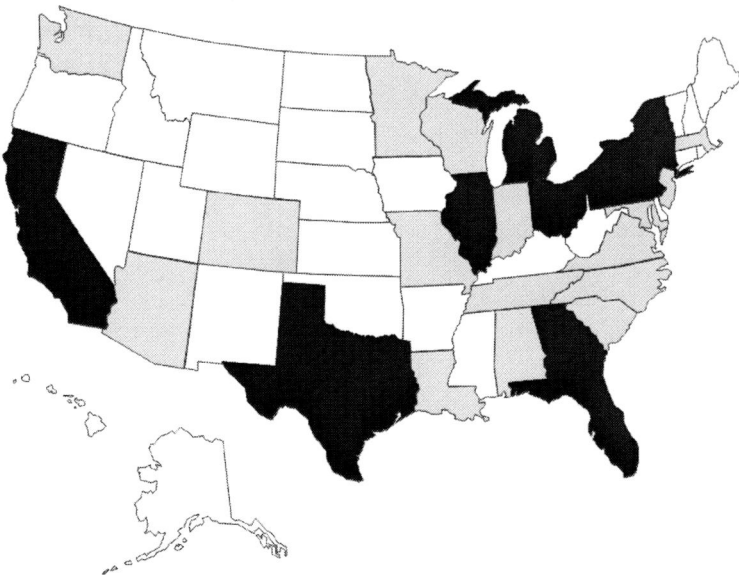

Figure 4: Population Density Map

Population Density Variances

Our nation's population is becoming more concentrated within smaller geographic areas (cities), creating a greater imbalance between the rural and metropolitan concerns/issues. Today, roughly 80% of the population lives in a city while the remaining 20% of the population lives in the rural areas. The current Electoral College method is not sensitive to this basic difference (see Winner Takes All).

Clearly, all states are not populated equally. Alaska, for example, is sparsely populated having a little more than 1.2 persons per square mile. New Jersey, on the other hand, is quite dense currently having 1189 people per square mile. People's values and concerns shift in relation to such density variations. Such values and concerns greatly affect how a citizen from a sparsely populated area views a candidate versus a citizen from a densely populated area.

There needs to be some device that helps level the field in terms of granting representation in a more equitable manner among all states. **We need a voting system that captures the popular vote while being sensitive to the regional concerns of our nation.** The execution of our present Electoral College is failing in that accountability.

In addition to the lack of representation that a national popular vote method provides, it can be argued that voter apathy could actually increase. If the pool of voters is on a national scale, it becomes easy for a voter to rationalize (realize?) that his/her vote means little. Such a method actually encourages voters to quietly disengage from the process.

The tables on the next pages, taken from www.wikipedia.com (Wikipedia, 2012), show how varied the population concentrations are among the nation's states. The first table lists the states in alphabetical order. The second table shows the state population densities (number of people per square mile or square kilometer) as they are ranked in descending order, from the densest to the sparsest.

Locate the state you live in and note its density ranking. Notice which states have similar densities as does your state. Have those states voted similarly to yours in past elections (compare the black and gray results on the bar graphs shown in the Appendix).

Table 2: Population Density by Alphabet

Rank	State	Population density
28	Alabama	94.65 inhabitants per square mile (36.54 /km^2)
51	Alaska	1.264 inhabitants per square mile (0.488 /km^2)
34	Arizona	57.05 inhabitants per square mile (22.03 /km^2)
35	Arkansas	56.43 inhabitants per square mile (21.79 /km^2)
12	California	241.7 inhabitants per square mile (93.3 /km^2)
38	Colorado	49.33 inhabitants per square mile (19.05 /km^2)
5	Connecticut	739.1 inhabitants per square mile (285.4 /km^2)
7	Delaware	464.3 inhabitants per square mile (179.3 /km^2)
1	District of Columbia	10,065 inhabitants per square mile (3,886 /km^2)
9	Florida	353.4 inhabitants per square mile (136.4 /km^2)
19	Georgia	169.5 inhabitants per square mile (65.4 /km^2)
14	Hawaii	214.1 inhabitants per square mile (82.7 /km^2)
45	Idaho	19.15 inhabitants per square mile (7.39 /km^2)
13	Illinois	231.5 inhabitants per square mile (89.4 /km^2)
17	Indiana	181.7 inhabitants per square mile (70.2 /km^2)
37	Iowa	54.81 inhabitants per square mile (21.16 /km^2)
41	Kansas	35.09 inhabitants per square mile (13.55 /km^2)
23	Kentucky	110.0 inhabitants per square mile (42.5 /km^2)
25	Louisiana	105.0 inhabitants per square mile (40.5 /km^2)
39	Maine	43.04 inhabitants per square mile (16.62 /km^2)
6	Maryland	596.3 inhabitants per square mile (230.2 /km^2)
4	Massachusetts	840.2 inhabitants per square mile (324.4 /km^2)
18	Michigan	173.9 inhabitants per square mile (67.1 /km^2)
32	Minnesota	67.14 inhabitants per square mile (25.92 /km^2)
33	Mississippi	63.50 inhabitants per square mile (24.52 /km^2)
29	Missouri	87.26 inhabitants per square mile (33.69 /km^2)
49	Montana	6.858 inhabitants per square mile (2.648 /km^2)
44	Nebraska	23.97 inhabitants per square mile (9.25 /km^2)
43	Nevada	24.80 inhabitants per square mile (9.58 /km^2)
22	New Hampshire	147.0 inhabitants per square mile (56.8 /km^2)
2	New Jersey	1,189 inhabitants per square mile (459 /km^2)
46	New Mexico	17.16 inhabitants per square mile (6.63 /km^2)
8	New York	412.3 inhabitants per square mile (159.2 /km^2)
16	North Carolina	198.2 inhabitants per square mile (76.5 /km^2)
48	North Dakota	9.916 inhabitants per square mile (3.829 /km^2)
11	Ohio	281.9 inhabitants per square mile (108.8 /km^2)
36	Oklahoma	55.22 inhabitants per square mile (21.32 /km^2)
40	Oregon	40.33 inhabitants per square mile (15.57 /km^2)
10	Pennsylvania	284.3 inhabitants per square mile (109.8 /km^2)
3	Rhode Island	1,006 inhabitants per square mile (388 /km^2)
20	South Carolina	155.4 inhabitants per square mile (60.0 /km^2)
47	South Dakota	10.86 inhabitants per square mile (4.19 /km^2)
21	Tennessee	155.4 inhabitants per square mile (60.0 /km^2)
27	Texas	98.07 inhabitants per square mile (37.87 /km^2)
42	Utah	34.30 inhabitants per square mile (13.24 /km^2)
31	Vermont	67.73 inhabitants per square mile (26.15 /km^2)
15	Virginia	204.5 inhabitants per square mile (79.0 /km^2)
26	Washington	102.6 inhabitants per square mile (39.6 /km^2)
30	West Virginia	77.06 inhabitants per square mile (29.75 /km^2)
24	Wisconsin	105.2 inhabitants per square mile (40.6 /km^2)
50	Wyoming	5.851 inhabitants per square mile (2.259 /km^2)

Table 3: Population Density by Rank

Rank	State	Population density
1	District of Columbia	10,065 inhabitants per square mile (3,886 /km²)
2	New Jersey	1,189 inhabitants per square mile (459 /km²)
3	Rhode Island	1,006 inhabitants per square mile (388 /km²)
4	Massachusetts	840.2 inhabitants per square mile (324.4 /km²)
5	Connecticut	739.1 inhabitants per square mile (285.4 /km²)
6	Maryland	596.3 inhabitants per square mile (230.2 /km²)
7	Delaware	464.3 inhabitants per square mile (179.3 /km²)
8	New York	412.3 inhabitants per square mile (159.2 /km²)
9	Florida	353.4 inhabitants per square mile (136.4 /km²)
10	Pennsylvania	284.3 inhabitants per square mile (109.8 /km²)
11	Ohio	281.9 inhabitants per square mile (108.8 /km²)
12	California	241.7 inhabitants per square mile (93.3 /km²)
13	Illinois	231.5 inhabitants per square mile (89.4 /km²)
14	Hawaii	214.1 inhabitants per square mile (82.7 /km²)
15	Virginia	204.5 inhabitants per square mile (79.0 /km²)
16	North Carolina	198.2 inhabitants per square mile (76.5 /km²)
17	Indiana	181.7 inhabitants per square mile (70.2 /km²)
18	Michigan	173.9 inhabitants per square mile (67.1 /km²)
19	Georgia	169.5 inhabitants per square mile (65.4 /km²)
20	South Carolina	155.4 inhabitants per square mile (60.0 /km²)
21	Tennessee	155.4 inhabitants per square mile (60.0 /km²)
22	New Hampshire	147.0 inhabitants per square mile (56.8 /km²)
23	Kentucky	110.0 inhabitants per square mile (42.5 /km²)
24	Wisconsin	105.2 inhabitants per square mile (40.6 /km²)
25	Louisiana	105.0 inhabitants per square mile (40.5 /km²)
26	Washington	102.6 inhabitants per square mile (39.6 /km²)
27	Texas	98.07 inhabitants per square mile (37.87 /km²)
28	Alabama	94.65 inhabitants per square mile (36.54 /km²)
29	Missouri	87.26 inhabitants per square mile (33.69 /km²)
30	West Virginia	77.06 inhabitants per square mile (29.75 /km²)
31	Vermont	67.73 inhabitants per square mile (26.15 /km²)
32	Minnesota	67.14 inhabitants per square mile (25.92 /km²)
33	Mississippi	63.50 inhabitants per square mile (24.52 /km²)
34	Arizona	57.05 inhabitants per square mile (22.03 /km²)
35	Arkansas	56.43 inhabitants per square mile (21.79 /km²)
36	Oklahoma	55.22 inhabitants per square mile (21.32 /km²)
37	Iowa	54.81 inhabitants per square mile (21.16 /km²)
38	Colorado	49.33 inhabitants per square mile (19.05 /km²)
39	Maine	43.04 inhabitants per square mile (16.62 /km²)
40	Oregon	40.33 inhabitants per square mile (15.57 /km²)
41	Kansas	35.09 inhabitants per square mile (13.55 /km²)
42	Utah	34.30 inhabitants per square mile (13.24 /km²)
43	Nevada	24.80 inhabitants per square mile (9.58 /km²)
44	Nebraska	23.97 inhabitants per square mile (9.25 /km²)
45	Idaho	19.15 inhabitants per square mile (7.39 /km²)
46	New Mexico	17.16 inhabitants per square mile (6.63 /km²)
47	South Dakota	10.86 inhabitants per square mile (4.19 /km²)
48	North Dakota	9.916 inhabitants per square mile (3.829 /km²)
49	Montana	6.858 inhabitants per square mile (2.648 /km²)
50	Wyoming	5.851 inhabitants per square mile (2.259 /km²)
51	Alaska	1.264 inhabitants per square mile (0.488 /km²)

City Voting

You have already seen how voter representation is lost on the state level when we use the Electoral College in its current format. If you're a Democrat, for example, and you're voting in the rural areas of the country, you may feel like your vote doesn't count for much when other voters go Republican and your representation gets lost. Your voting voice essentially disappears!

However, the reverse effect occurs in the city as well. Let's assume that you're voting Republican in one of the larger urban areas that vote Democratic. If the city population is large enough, the Democratic vote could sway the entire state results.

Here are some graphs to illustrate the point that a lot of city voting representation is not captured in the Electoral College, as it is currently used. There are 10 cities shown below in the graphs that identify the percentage of Democratic and Republican voting in 2012. These and 40 more results are shown in the Appendix. Each city is shown according to the major county it is in, which is identified in the parenthesis after each city name. The percentages do not always equal 100% because other candidate voting has been subtracted from the total figures used here.

It can be argued that these graphs are not entirely accurate, then, as the vote count may not be all of the votes cast within a city's boundaries. For example, some city counties include portions of surrounding suburbs. San Diego is a good example of this. Other city counties may exclude portions considered to be within that city's metropolitan area. New York's King County would be a good example of this limitation. However, the story doesn't shift much if you are able to count all of the city dweller voting and compare those results with what is depicted here.

The point of these graphs is to show that much of the city voting population does not get represented by the current use of our Electoral College. You'll see that much of the population votes for the candidate that loses its state. Therefore, these voters are never represented in the Electoral College as it is currently used.

An interesting statistic, looking only at the statistics shown in these graphs (including those in the Appendix), is that 42.2% of the city voters cast their ballots for candidates that did not carry their state. These voters did not receive representation in the current Electoral College process!

In case you're wondering, 26 of these cities are in states that awarded their electoral votes to Obama with the other 24 cities being in states that went to Romney. Consequently, one cannot simply say that cities always vote democratic or that city voting carries the state's choice.

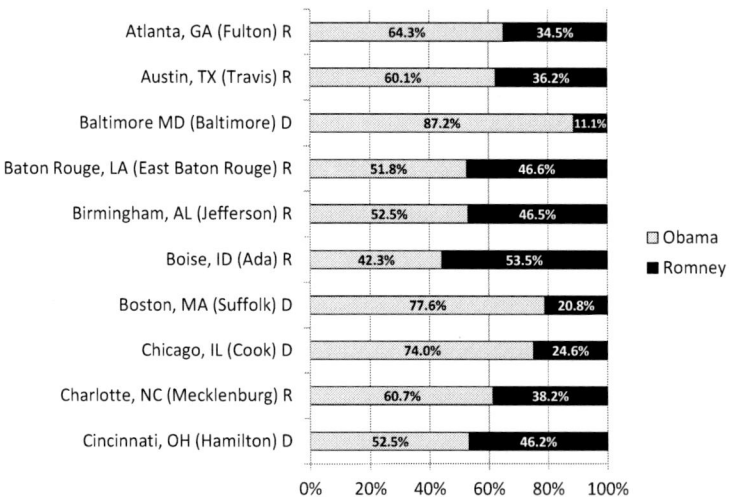

City	Obama	Romney
Atlanta, GA (Fulton) R	64.3%	34.5%
Austin, TX (Travis) R	60.1%	36.2%
Baltimore MD (Baltimore) D	87.2%	11.1%
Baton Rouge, LA (East Baton Rouge) R	51.8%	46.6%
Birmingham, AL (Jefferson) R	52.5%	46.5%
Boise, ID (Ada) R	42.3%	53.5%
Boston, MA (Suffolk) D	77.6%	20.8%
Chicago, IL (Cook) D	74.0%	24.6%
Charlotte, NC (Mecklenburg) R	60.7%	38.2%
Cincinnati, OH (Hamilton) D	52.5%	46.2%

Figure 5: 2012 City Voting Graph

CONGRESSIONAL DISTRICTS

There has been some discussion about how electoral votes should be decided by ballots cast within congressional districts. This is not a good idea! Two concerns surface with this approach. One is the concern over representation. The other concern is about opening the door to manipulation. Let's talk about the issue of fair and balanced representation first.

We're fortunate in that we already have good examples to examine to see how congressional voting works. Maine and Nebraska have been using the congressional district voting approach for some time. Maine began doing so in 1972. Twenty years later, 1992, Nebraska decided to do the same.

While I'm criticizing the approach, I also appreciate the fact that theirs is a better approach when compared to the other 48 states. At least there's an acknowledgement that splitting the vote within a state is a better idea than having a winner-takes-all strategy.

Here's how it works. The electoral votes are allocated to a candidate that wins the popular vote within a state's congressional district. Maine has four congressional districts and Nebraska has five. Theoretically, Maine could split its electoral votes in a 1 to 3 or a 2 to 2 combination. Similarly, Nebraska could split its votes in combinations of 1 to 4 or 2 to 3. That seems fair.

What does history reveal? Maine has never split it electoral votes since 1972. Nebraska split its votes 1 to 4 in the 2008 presidential election when its second congressional district voted for Obama instead of McCain. That's not a lot of movement.

The concern is that voters, selecting a candidate who does not win the most popular votes within a state, do not get any representation in that state's electoral vote tabulation. To illustrate this, the following graph shows the percentages and number of voters casting their ballots for either Obama or Romney in the 2012 election in the states of Maine and Nebraska.

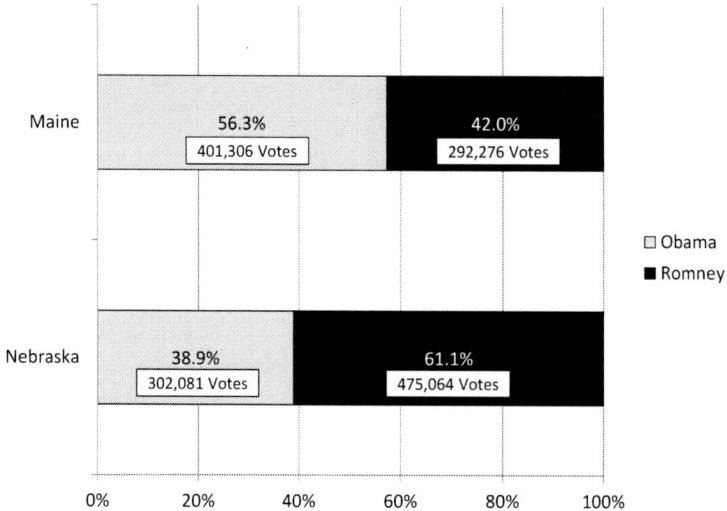

Figure 6: 2012 Maine & Nebraska Voting

A total of 594,357 voters, or 40.4%, within these two states did not have electoral vote representation in the 2012 election.

While the attempt to use a more equitable and representative Electoral College process was followed, a significant number of voters were disenfranchised in the most recent election. The flaws still persist and the people's choice is not fully representative of the ballots cast.

Since we're looking at history, the following two graphs show how the votes in Maine and Nebraska were cast for the years 1980 through 2008. Remember, only Nebraska split off one electoral vote in 2008. All of the other voting was for one candidate within each state.

Maine

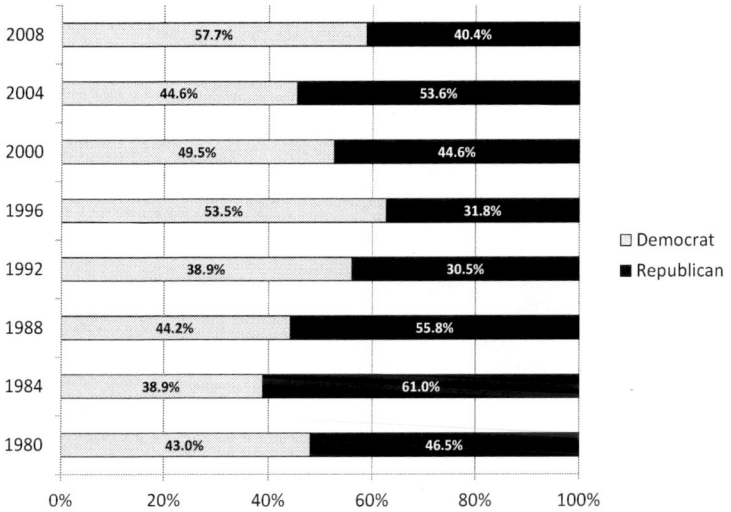

	Democrat	Republican
2008	57.7%	40.4%
2004	44.6%	53.6%
2000	49.5%	44.6%
1996	53.5%	31.8%
1992	38.9%	30.5%
1988	44.2%	55.8%
1984	38.9%	61.0%
1980	43.0%	46.5%

Figure 7: 1980 – 2008 Maine Voting

Nebraska

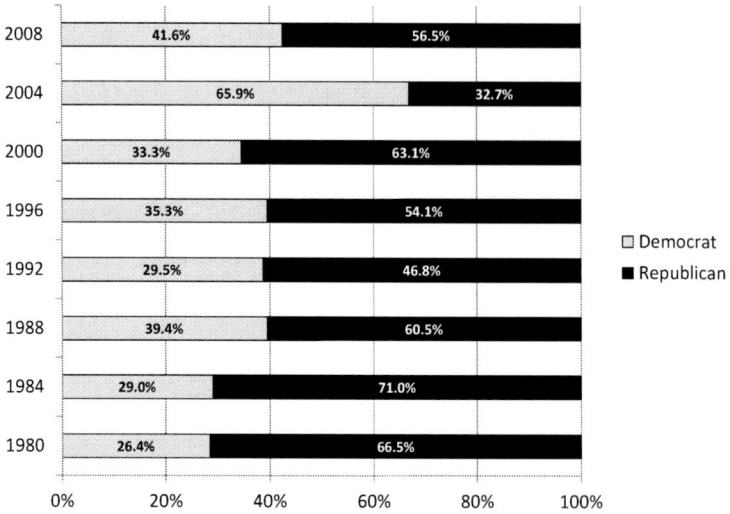

Figure 8: 1980 – 2008 Nebraska Voting

Now let's turn our attention to the second concern, which is that of manipulation.

Remember how I mentioned that our voting mechanism (the Electoral College) should be fair and balanced? Congressional districts are notorious for being manipulated by whoever represents them. It's called gerrymandering. The following description, taken from www.wikipedia.com, describes how the process and the word came into being:

> The word gerrymander (originally written Gerry-
> mander) was used for the first time in the Boston
> Gazette on March 26, 1812. The word was created
> in reaction to a redrawing of Massachusetts state
> Senate election districts under the then-governor
> Elbridge Gerry (1744–1814). In 1812, Governor
> Gerry signed a bill that redistricted Massachusetts
> to benefit his Democratic-Republican Party. When
> mapped, one of the contorted districts in the
> Boston area was said to resemble the shape of a
> salamander. The term was a portmanteau
> [combination] of the governor's last name and the
> word salamander.
>
> Appearing with the term, and helping to spread and
> sustain its popularity, was a political cartoon
> depicting a strange animal with claws, wings and a
> dragon-like head satirizing the map of the odd-
> shaped district. This cartoon was most likely drawn
> by Elkanah Tisdale, an early 19th-century painter,
> designer, and engraver who was living in Boston at
> the time.

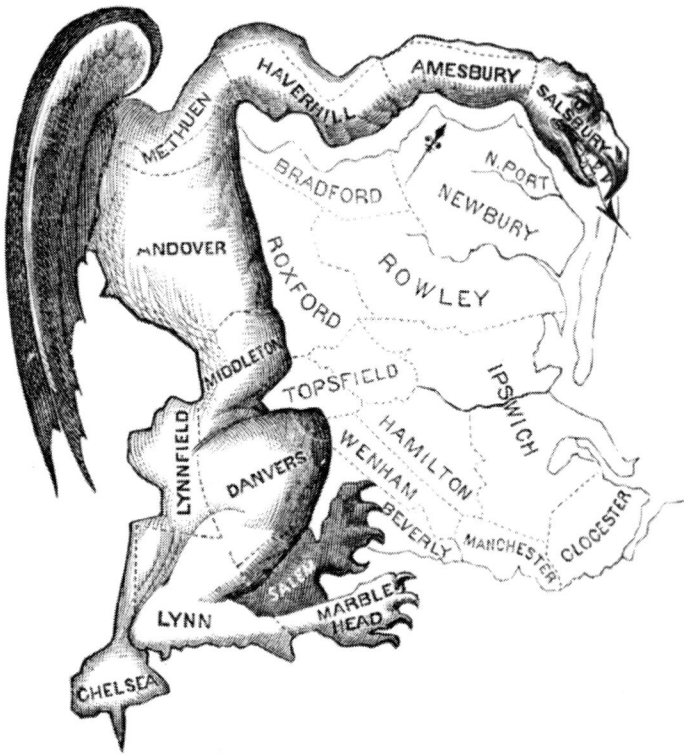

Figure 9: Gerrymander Cartoon

The word gerrymander was reprinted numerous
times in Federalist newspapers in Massachusetts,
New England, and nationwide during the
remainder of 1812. This suggests some organized
activity of the Federalists to disparage Governor
Gerry, in particular, and the growing Democratic -
Republican Party in general.

Gerrymandering soon began to be used to describe not only the original Massachusetts example, but also other cases of district-shape manipulation for partisan gain in other states. According to the Oxford English Dictionary, the word's acceptance was marked by its first publication in a dictionary (1848) and in an encyclopedia (1868).

In other words, congressional districts are often constructed to give the most favor to the political party that currently holds the most influence. These lines are redrawn whenever a new national census is taken. The next redrawing of congressional district borders will occur in 2020. It is one of the primary reasons that incumbent representatives are so confident they will win the vote, term after term, to retain their seat in the House of Representatives. Such manipulation to bend to a controlling power is not a good basis for forming a voting mechanism for our nation's Electoral College.

The following page shows a congressional district that has been subjected to gerrymandering. There are 19 more shown in the Appendix. 10 of them are currently held by Democrats and 10 by Republicans. The maps are taken from the www.NationalAtlas.gov Web site (NationalAtlas, 2012). Notice how convoluted they are (salamanders?) as they strive to include the party of choice voters and exclude others. Words like *Control*, *Manipulation*, and *Unfair* should spring to mind.

Alabama's sixth Congressional District is currently held by Republicans.

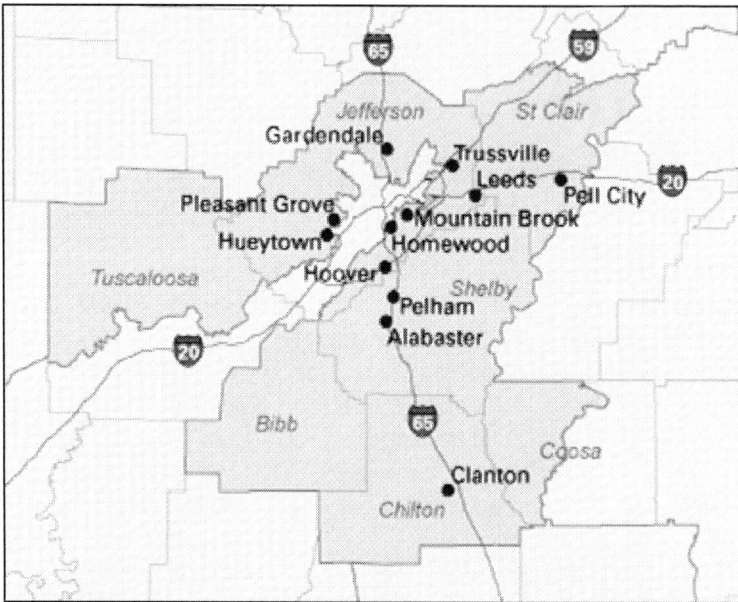

Figure 10: Alabama Congressional District #6

EQUAL VOICE VOTING METHOD

The truth is that neither our current Electoral College nor a popular vote method captures or well reflects the will of the citizens of our United States in a clear, unambiguous way. It is time to modify the Electoral College!

What is the answer? Equal Voice Voting is an alternative voting method that capitalizes on the wisdom of our Founding Fathers and incorporates both a popular vote as well as a geographic representation for our presidential vote allocation.

Equal Voice voting makes every vote count!

An example of our Founding Fathers' concern put into action is illustrated (Getty Images, 2013) in how our nation's Congress is formed. The House of Representatives is populated with representatives from each state, according to each state's current population.

There are 435 representatives, each representing a portion of the population from his/her state.

Figure 11: House of Representative Depiction

Giving balance to this method of representation, each state also is represented by two senators, regardless of the size of the state. This mechanism ensures each state has an equal voice in the United States Senate.

Each state has two senators.

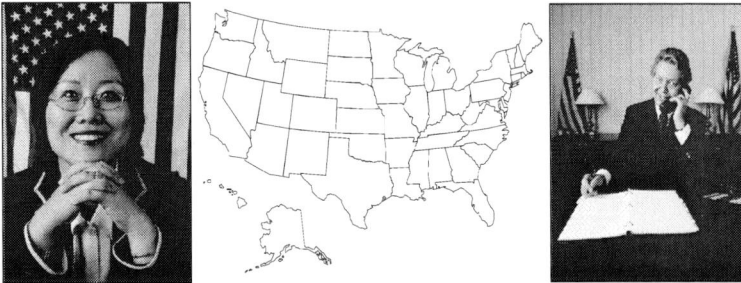

Figure 12: Senate Depiction

The Electoral College combines the 435 votes for every member of the House of Representatives plus three for Washington's District of Columbia for a total representative count of 438. This number is then combined with 100 to correlate with the members of the Senate, giving us a total 538 electoral votes.

The Equal Voice (EV) voting method gives representation for each state's popular vote which, in turn, causes the state's electoral votes to be divided among the candidates. The EV voting method provides the results desired as it:

- Allocates representation to the popular vote
- Allocates representation to the geographic concerns
- Encourages everyone to vote, suppressing voter apathy
- Prevents voter disenfranchisement
- Is easy to understand
- Does not need a constitutional amendment

The following is a description of the EV voting method for allocating our votes to gain greater representation. It is designed to give greater representation to everyone across the nation and to every state. Hopefully, it will encourage a more vigorous voting response from our citizens.

Determine the Popular Vote Value (PVV)

Step 1.   Total the state's popular votes.

Step 2.   Divide by the state's electoral votes.

The result is called the Popular Vote Value (PVV). The PVV is rounded to the nearest whole number. For example, using the state of Ohio, the popular vote (all ballots for all candidates) in this past election (2012) was 5,580,822. Dividing that number by 18 reduces the result to 310,045.66. That number is rounded to 310,046 as the PVV.

Formula to determine Popular Vote Value (PVV):

$$\frac{\text{State Election's Popular Votes}}{\text{State's Electoral Votes}} = \text{PVV (Popular Vote Value)}$$

Determine the state's Equal Voice Votes (EVVs) for each candidate. Divide the candidate's popular vote by the Popular Vote Value (PVV). The result is rounded to the nearest whole number. For example, using the PVV example above, Ohio's popular vote for Obama was 2,827,621. Dividing that number by 310,046 (PVV) results in 9.12. The number is rounded down to 9 EVVs. The popular votes for Romney were 2,661,407. This number divided by 310,046 gives a result of 8.58. This number would be rounded up to the whole number of 9 for the candidate's EVVs.

$$\frac{\text{Candidate's State Popular Votes}}{\text{PVV}} = \text{EVVs (Candidate's Equal Voice Votes)}$$

Adjustment Rules

Rounding votes either up or down to determine EVVs may cause the total to exceed or fall short of the 538 number established by the Electoral College. The following rules are required to ensure the aggregate total of EVVs equals 538 and are correct for each state:

1. A candidate's popular votes must equal the PVV before rounding can be used. For example, if the PVV is 250,000 and a candidate's popular vote for a state is 150,000, no rounding can occur, even though the typical rounding rules would round up to equal one EVV. That candidate would receive no EVV. third party candidate are the most likely to experience this adjustment rule.

2. Each state's EVVs must equal the allotted votes established by the Electoral College. For example, if a state's Electoral College vote number is ten (such as Maryland, Minnesota, Missouri, and Wisconsin) and either fewer or more EVVs are won by that state, an adjustment must be made. To make an EVV adjustment, do the following:

   a. If the EVV count for a state is too many, remove one EVV from the candidate who has won the fewest popular votes.

   b. If the EVV count for a state is too few, add one EVV to the candidate who has won the most popular votes.

   Note: Typically, this is only a one vote adjustment for a given state. However, some rare situations may require two votes to be added or subtracted.

Determine the Winner

Determine the number of electoral votes.

Total the Equal Voice Votes (EVVs) for each candidate from each state. The winner of the most EVVs wins the election.

Example (Ohio 2012)

Step 1. Total the state's popular votes for the election.

The total state popular vote (all ballots for all candidates) was 5,580,822.

Step 2. Determine the state's Popular Vote Value (PVV).

Divide the state's election's popular votes by its electoral votes. 5,580,822 divided by 18 = 310,046 state PVV (rounded value).

Step 3. Determine the number of the state's electoral votes.

Divide the state's popular vote for each candidate in the current election by the state's PVV. Electoral votes are rounded up or down to the nearest Popular Vote Value.

Popular vote for Romney= 2,661,407
Popular vote for Obama= 2,827,621
Dividing each by 310,046 = Equal Voice Votes:
   Romney's = 8.58 – rounded up to 9 EVVs
   Obama's = 9.12 – rounded down to 9 EVVs

Comparing EV Voting to the Current Voting Method

The following graph is shown here to compare the 2012 election between the popular votes, electoral votes cast, and how these same elections would fare under the Equal Voice voting method. The gray bars depict the results for the Democrats; the black bars depict the results for the Republicans. More graphs are shown in the Appendix. Some graphs shown in the Appendix use white bars for third party candidates, when needed.

As you review the charts, notice how close in height the popular votes (solid bars) compare to the Equal Voice Votes (vertical striped bars). Then compare these heights with the Electoral College results depicted here with the horizontal striped bars. Typically, these bars vary significantly from the other two.

The 2012 election shows that Obama won by a large margin, when considering the Electoral College votes. Yet, his victory was only won by a 3.8% popular vote margin. The EVVs won by both candidates clearly shows a more equal representation.

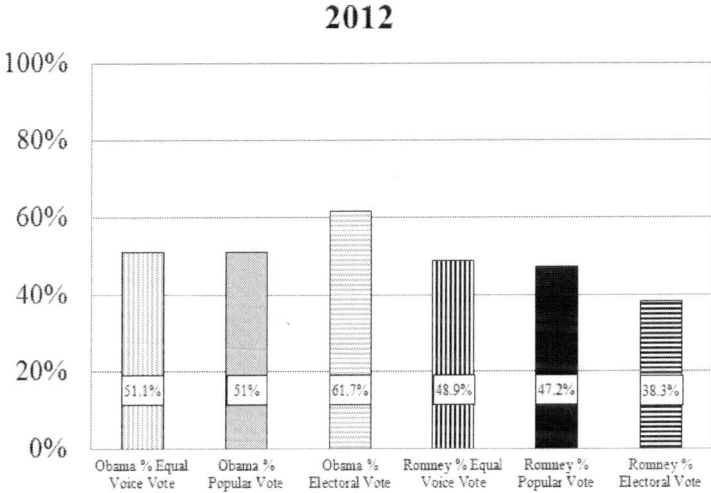

Figure 13: 2012 EVV, Popular & Electoral Votes

Variances between parties

Popular Votes (solid bars) = 51%:47.2% = 3.8%
Electoral Votes (horizontal striped bars) =
     61.7%:38.3% = 23.4%
EVVs (vertical striped bars) = 51.1%:48.9% = 2.2%
Variance between EVVs and Popular Votes:
     Democrat = 51.1%:51% = 0.1%
     Republican = 48.9%:47.2% = 1.7%

Electoral Vote Variance Summaries

Fair Warning: Remember how I told you I can be a bit
geeky? Well, this section digs into numbers a little deeper.
If you're not a *numbers* person, feel free to skip ahead to
the next section.

The tables below display the two major party voting results
by showing the variances between the electoral and
popular votes for all nine of the example elections (1980 –
2012). These variances are compared between the two
major parties. The first table shows the current comparison
and the second table shows the results if the Electoral
College would have been replaced with Equal Voice during
those presidential election years.

Notice that the two tables employ a different array of
percentages. The first table extends from 0% to 45% (along
the left side), while the second table's array extends from
0% to 4.5%. The first table shows that the variance of
electoral votes from the popular vote is rather extreme;
whereas, the second table shows the variances are often
equal or vary only slightly.

Table 4: Variances of Electoral Votes Compared to Popular Votes

	Democrat	Republican
1980	32.7%	39.2%
1984	38.5%	38.5%
1988	25.3%	25.3%
1992	25.5%	6.5%
1996	20.4%	11.9%
2000	0.8%	1.8%
2004	1.5%	2.9%
2008	14.9%	13.4%
2012	10.3%	10.3%

Equal Voice Voting

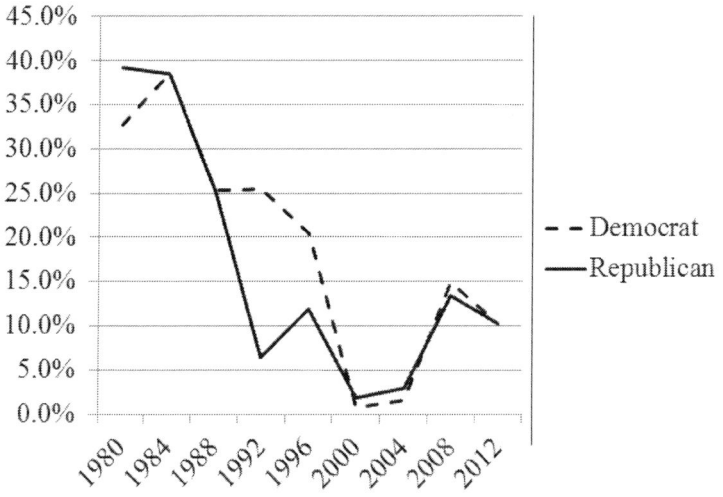

Figure 14: Electoral College Voting Variances

Ideally, the variances between popular and the final election results should be minimal. Notice that the scale used in this graph ranges from 0% to only 4.5% (compared to 0% to 45% for the current Electoral College method). The EV voting method shows the variance remains less than 4.5% for Reagan in the 1980 race and less than half of that for the other candidates and contests. The current Electoral College method, on the other hand, exceeds 10% most of the time.

Table 5: Variances of Equal Voice Votes
Compared to Popular Votes

	Democrat	Republican
1980	0.4%	4.1%
1984	0.4%	0.4%
1988	0.2%	0.2%
1992	1.7%	1.7%
1996	1.6%	2.1%
2000	0%	1%
2004	0%	1%
2008	0.8%	0.7%
2012	0.1%	1.7%

Equal Voice Voting

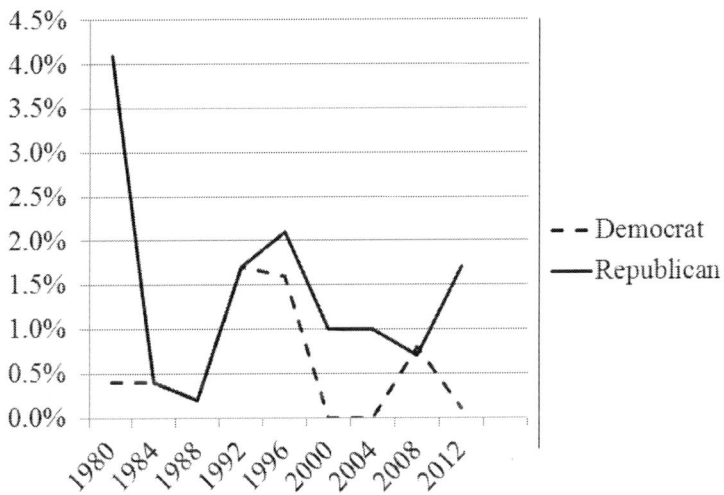

Figure 15: Voting Variances Using Equal Voting

MEDIA COVERAGE

Another aspect of our current voting process is how the news media reports the results. Obviously, there was much confusion over the Florida results in the 2000 election; but the concern goes further than that. Often, the Eastern states' results are reported early in the day (relatively speaking) while those citizens in the West may not have yet voted. Often a candidate is declared a winner as a foregone conclusion before the polls are closed in the West, effectively encouraging the voting citizenry in the more westerly regions of our country to not vote – forfeiting their right – forfeiting their voice. Essentially, this process fuels the voting apathy that undercuts our very democratic process.

The early reporting is not simply a fault of our news media. It is the media's job to keep our populace informed and, on Election Day, voting results are what everyone is interested in – it's news. Changing how the news is reported on Election Day may significantly address the early winner declaration problem.

What if that same media tenacity actually worked to encourage people to vote? What if early reporting could not spring to an early conclusion? What if the news gave a running sense of how each region's voting hung in the balance and actually encouraged everyone to get out and vote *because their vote counted*?

While not having actual results to point to, I am suggesting that the totaling of a candidate's EV votes (EVVs) cannot be done early. To that end I have selected four states, one in each time zone, to simulate how voting tallies for the 2012 election could have played out. Remember, this is a speculative set of scenarios; however, it does point to how time is required for each state to declare a final tally.

The four states selected are New Hampshire, Alabama, Colorado, and Washington. The popular votes were counted according to their respective counties. I have made the assumption that voting precincts' results would be accumulated on a county-by-county basis. It is understood that vote counting may go rapidly or slowly, depending on the support and the number of people involved. However, I assumed that counties with larger populations would count votes faster than small ones simply because they would have a larger staff to do the counting.

For example, I only created four categories of counties: 1 to 10,000 voters, 10,001 to 75,000, 75,001 to 250,000 voters, and counties with 250,001 + voters. Each county size was further assumed able to count votes at a different rate, as the table below shows:

Table 6: Example Vote Count Rates

County Size	# of Votes Captured	Rate of Vote Counting per Hour
Small	1-10,000	1,000 Votes
Medium	10,001-75,000	7,500 Votes
Large	75,001-250,000	40,000 Votes
Extra Large	250,000+	80,000 Votes

This table represents a lot of assumptions, but with these assumptions in mind, look at how this fictitious vote counting could be done. The key point to consider is the percentage of votes that must be counted before a final tally can be certain.

The following four tables depict each state, showing the time lapse in increments of 30 minutes (half hour). The votes cast for each candidate is shown in the next two columns on a cumulative basis. The total percentage of votes cast is then shown in the second and third columns. This is followed by a tally of the EV Votes (EVVs) for each candidate (third party candidates did not provide significant results to be shown for this exercise).

Typically, if a candidate wins or loses a state, it is determined early in the process, often when less than half of the votes have been counted. In these scenarios, you'll see that cannot be done. This is because it is not a winner-takes-all type of voting. Each candidate wins EVVs, causing the assessment to be extended time-wise from the current experience.

The EV voting method relies on the Popular Vote Value (PVV), which is determined using the total number of popular votes cast in a state. This is an unknown factor while the votes are being gathered and counted. Therefore, any estimates would probably rely on the voting experience of the previous presidential election. This approach was used for this simulation. Once the true popular vote is realized, the factor would be adjusted and revisions made to the EVVs. This kind of adjustment affects both candidates equally, so the vote tally in the sense of which candidate is ahead or behind, will not change, though the EVVs will. This situation appeared for Alabama and Washington and is discussed when those tables are presented.

New Hampshire polls closed at 8:00 p.m. Eastern Standard Time (EST). That is the zero hour in the first table. The remaining three states also close their polls at 8:00 p.m., relative to their corresponding time zones.

- Eastern Standard Time (EST)   New Hampshire
- Central Standard Time (CST)   Alabama
- Mountain Standard Time (MST) Colorado
- Pacific Standard Time (PST)   Washington

It was also assumed that some vote counting may have occurred in each state before their polls closed. Therefore, their zero hour tallies show a portion of votes counted, ranging from 10.6% to 14.49%.

New Hampshire: This is the smallest of the four states. Assuming that the vote counting would be slower due to fewer people involved in the process, the vote count extended into the ninth hour (5:00 a.m.). That may or not be accurate, but the key point in these results is that the total EVVs for both candidates could not be determined until almost 80% of the vote was counted, which would be close to midnight on the East coast! The gray highlight below shows when both candidates had successfully won their respective EVVs.

Table 7: New Hampshire Example Vote Count Rates

New Hampshire			
Hours	**Vote %**	**EVVs**	
	Counted	**Obama**	**Romney**
0	11.64%	0	0
0.5	23.17%	0	0
1	34.70%	0	0
1.5	46.23%	1	0
2	54.95%	1	1
2.5	63.21%	1	1
3	71.47%	2	1
3.5	79.73%	2	2
4	86.36%	2	2
4.5	90.99%	2	2
5	93.37%	2	2
5.5	94.74%	2	2
6	95.99%	2	2
6.5	96.90%	2	2
7	97.81%	2	2
7.5	98.31%	2	2
8	98.77%	2	2
8.5	99.22%	2	2
9	99.68%	2	2

Alabama: This state has the most counties of the four states selected. Vote counting extended into the eighth hour (4:00 a.m.). That may or not be accurate, but the key point in these results is that the total EVVs for both candidates could not be determined until more than 87% of the vote was counted, which would be close to midnight in the Central Standard Time zone! The gray highlight below shows when both candidates had successfully won their respective EVVs.

Table 8: Alabama Example Vote Count Rates

Alabama			
Hours	Vote % Counted	EVVs	
		Obama	Romney
0	14.49%	0	0
0.5	28.99%	0	0
1	43.48%	1	2
1.5	57.19%	2	3
2	67.90%	2	4
2.5	76.22%	3	4
3	83.17%	3	4
3.5	87.68%	3	5
4	90.96%	3	5
4.5	93.38%	3	5
5	95.40%	3	5
5.5	96.71%	3	5
6	97.91%	3	5
6.5	98.75%	3	5
7	99.38%	3	5
7.5	99.81%	3	5
8	100%	3	5

An adjustment had to be made once all of the voting was completed, noting that the Popular Vote Value was decreased from the PPV used from the previous election. This caused Romney to earn one more EVV. However it would not have become apparent until 2:00 a.m. even if the correct PPV were used! Again, there is no danger of one candidate exceeding another's EVV count due to this adjustment.

Colorado: Colorado was noted as a swing state in the last election (2012). The vote count ended around 5 am, Mountain Standard Time. Actual vote counting for this kind of scenario could easily be different, but, again, the key point in these results is that the total EVVs for both candidates could not be determined until most of the votes were counted. In this simulation, more than 90% of the vote was needed before a final determination could be identified! The gray highlight below shows when both candidates had successfully won their respective EVVs.

Table 9: Colorado Example Vote Count Rates

Colorado			
Hours	Vote % Counted	EVVs	
		Obama	Romney
0	14.12%	0	0
0.5	28.18%	1	1
1	42.17%	2	2
1.5	55.33%	3	2
2	66.79%	3	3
2.5	77.76%	4	3
3	86.01%	4	4
3.5	90.53%	5	4
4	94.30%	5	4
4.5	95.44%	5	4
5	96.45%	5	4
5.5	97.41%	5	4
6	98.36%	5	4
6.5	99.26%	5	4
7	99.75%	5	4
7.5	99.85%	5	4
8	99.92%	5	4
8.5	99.97%	5	4
9	100%	5	4

Washington: Washington is the most populous state of the four chosen. Consequently, the scenario depicted below took longer than the previous three. The vote count finished at 7:30 a.m., Pacific Standard Time, with the EVV determination for the candidates occurring just 90 minutes prior to that. Actual vote counting for this kind of scenario could easily be different, but, again, the key point in these results is that the total EVVs for both candidates could not be determined until most of the votes were counted. In this simulation, more than 96% of the vote was needed before a final determination could be identified! The gray highlight below shows when both candidates had successfully won their respective EVVs.

Table 10: Washington Example Vote Count Rates

Washington			
Hours	**Vote %**	**EVVs**	
	Counted	**Obama**	**Romney**
0	10.62%	0	0
0.5	21.00%	1	1
1	31.35%	2	2
1.5	41.45%	2	2
2	50.23%	3	3
2.5	58.31%	4	3
3	65.21%	4	3
3.5	71.55%	4	4
4	76.34%	5	4
4.5	79.53%	5	4
5	82.32%	5	4
5.5	84.53%	5	4
6	86.48%	5	4
6.5	88.33%	5	4
7	90.12%	6	4
8.5	91.86%	6	4
9	93.56%	6	4
9.5	95.09%	6	4
10	96.54%	6	5
10.5	97.98%	6	5
11	99.41%	6	5
11.5	100%	6	5

An adjustment had to be made because the voter turn-out was less in 2012, causing Washington's PVV to decrease, allowing one more EV to be awarded to each candidate. The final EV tally would have been seven for Obama and five for Romney. As was noted earlier such adjustment does not cause one candidate to surpass another because both candidates are affected equally. No adjustment was needed when the actual PVV was determined for Colorado.

Final Scenario Summary: The following table shows all four states in the simulated voting just presented individually. The light gray highlights remain to show when the candidates' EVVs could be determined within the time frame. You'll notice that the adjustment changes are included with the changed EVV numbers in the parenthesis. The total columns on the far right are the final vote tallies for all four of these states. Among these four states, the EV voting method shows the candidates are tied at 17 EVVs each.

The intent is to show that determining a winner can be a longer process than what we currently experience. Consequently, the reporting of the process also would be extended, emphasizing the importance of each individual vote. While some may rush to predict the voting outcome, it may prove to be foolish. Rather, the news media could capitalize on the suspense that may ensue since the Electoral College, using the Equal Voice voting method, would closely follow the popular vote. Should that be close, the final outcome would be suspenseful to the end – which may well mean the early morning hours of the next day.

Table 11: Example States Vote Count Summary

Hours	New Hampshire EVVs Obama	New Hampshire EVVs Romney	Alabama EVVs Obama	Alabama EVVs Romney	Colorado EVVs Obama	Colorado EVVs Romney	Washington EVVs Obama	Washington EVVs Romney	Total EVVs Obama	Total EVVs Romney
0	0	0							0	0
0.5	0	0							0	0
1	0	0	0	0					0	0
1.5	1	0	0	0					1	0
2	1	1	1	2					2	3
2.5	1	1	2	3					4	5
3	2	1	2	4	0	0			6	6
3.5	2	2	3	4	1	1			9	9
4	2	2	3	4	2	2	0	0	10	11
4.5	2	2	3	5	3	2	1	1	11	12
5	2	2	3	5	3	3	2	2	12	14
5.5	2	2	3	5	4	3	2	2	14	14
6	2	2	3	5	4	4	3	3	14	14
6.5	2	2	3	5	5	4	4	3	15	15
7	2	2	3	5	5	4	4	4	15	15
7.5	2	2	3	5	5	4	5	4	16	16
8	2	2	3	5	5	4 (5)	5	4	16	16
8.5	2	2	3	5	5	4 (5)	5	4	16	16
9					5	4 (5)	5	4	16	16
10					5	4 (5)	6	4	16	16
10.5					5	4 (5)	6	4	16	16
11					5	4 (5)	6	4	16	16
11.5					5	4 (5)	6	4	16	16
12							6 (7)	5	17	17
12.5							6 (7)	5	17	17
13							6 (7)	5	17	17
13.5								5	17	17

EQUAL VOICE VOTING ADVANTAGES

The following is a list of reasons to use the Equal Voice
(EV) voting method:

- It captures the geographic representation for each
  state.

- It captures the popular vote representation for each
  state.

- It does not disenfranchise voters.

- It encourages citizens to vote as their voice is not lost
  amidst the dominant party voting in their state.

- It encourages the news media to not declare an early
  winner, yet increases the amount of election news to be
  reported as states report in with their respective vote
  tallies.

- It creates more election news to be reported, enticing
  voters to be more involved in the voting process as the
  results are reported.

- It is based on simple mathematics, so it is easy to
  implement.

- It retains the intent of our nation's Founding Fathers.

- Third (or more) party candidate electoral votes are
  counted and remain in the system.

- The large number of votes is reduced to a manageable
  number – retaining that aspect of the present Electoral
  College system.

- It encourages the candidates to campaign in all regions
  and address all issues, encouraging greater
  accountability to our nation's concerns.

Better Representation

As was seen in the 2000 election, when the popular vote ignores the geographic representation of our country, a true representation of our United States is not found in the present Electoral College system. Yet, the popular vote and geographic representation difference is one of the fundamental concerns our Founding Fathers had when they established our congressional representation to reflect the concerns of the heavily populated areas as well as those that are more rural.

The major contention here is that if voters think their ballots can make a difference, there will be a greater voter turn-out during election time. It can be argued that greater involvement by our citizenry and a weakened ability by our news media to pre-declare a winner causes greater representation/sensitivity to our nation's conscience during this critical voting process.

Election Stories

A depiction of our United States and a table is provided below to further illustrate how the EV voting method could have made a difference in the 2012 election. The past nine elections are also shown in the Appendix, showing how they would be counted according to each state and showing their respective popular votes and the total EVVs.

2012 Presidential Election

Look at the map: The map of the electoral vote state wins below appears balanced (Romney winning 24 states, Obama 26 states and Washington D.C.). However, Obama won by a 24% margin (332 electoral votes vs. 206 for Romney) using the current Electoral College voting method.

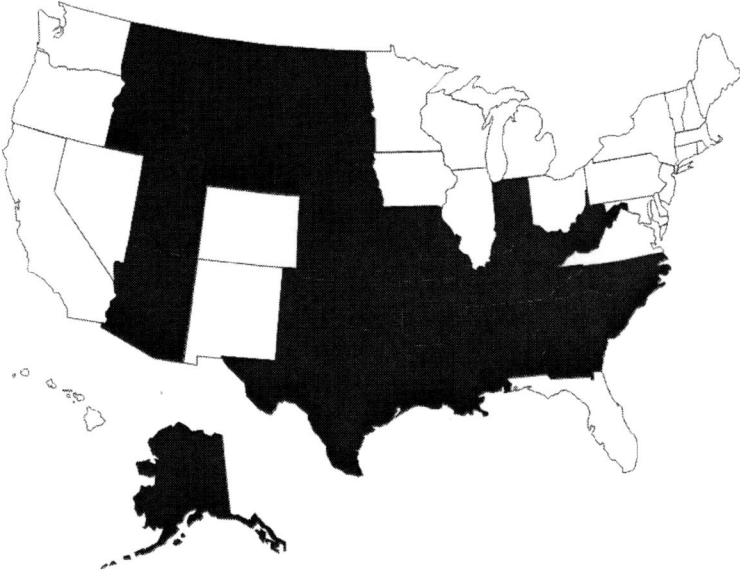

Figure 16: 2012 Presidential Election Map

Things to consider: Capturing the votes using the EV method reflects the balance revealed by the popular vote. Obama still wins the election, but the margin is reduced to a 1.86% margin with Obama winning by only 10 EVVs.

Nine states (highlighted in gray in the next table) tied in the number of EVVs. Two states and Washington D.C. (highlighted in black in the next table) awarded all of their EVVs to one candidate. The apparent mandate shown with our current Electoral College method disappears, providing more accurate data for everyone concerned to evaluate the results.

Table 12: 2012 Example Election Results

States	Popular Vote	Electoral Votes	PVV	Obama	Obama EVVs	Romney	Romney EVVs
AL	2074338	9	230482	3.45	3	5.45	6
AK	300495	3	100165	1.22	1	1.64	2
AZ	2306559	11	209687	4.89	5	5.88	6
AR	1069468	6	178245	2.21	2	3.63	4
CA	13038547	55	237064	33.13	34	20.42	21
CO	2569217	9	285469	4.63	5	4.15	4
CT	1558993	7	222713	4.06	4	2.85	3
DE	413890	3	137963	1.76	2	1.20	1
DC	293764	3	97921	2.73	3	0.22	0
FL	8490162	29	292764	14.47	15	14.22	14
GA	3900050	16	243753	7.28	7	8.53	9
HI	434697	4	108674	2.82	3	1.11	1
ID	656742	4	164186	1.30	1	2.56	3
IL	5244174	20	262209	11.52	12	8.14	8
IN	2624534	11	238594	4.83	5	5.95	6
IA	1582180	6	263697	3.12	3	2.77	3
KS	1159971	6	193329	2.28	2	3.58	4
KY	1797212	8	224652	3.02	3	4.84	5
LA	1994065	8	249258	3.25	3	4.62	5
ME	713180	4	178295	2.25	2	1.64	2
MD	2707327	10	270733	6.20	6	3.59	4
MA	3167767	11	287979	6.67	7	4.13	4
MI	4740250	16	296266	8.66	9	7.14	7
MN	2936561	10	293656	5.27	6	4.50	4
MS	1285584	6	214264	2.63	3	3.32	3
MO	2757323	10	275732	4.44	4	5.38	6
MT	484048	3	161349	1.25	1	1.66	2
NE	794379	5	158876	1.90	2	2.99	3
NV	1014918	6	169153	3.14	3	2.74	3
NH	710972	4	177743	2.08	2	1.86	2
NJ	3645887	14	260421	8.15	8	5.68	6
NM	783757	5	156751	2.65	3	2.14	2
NY	7061925	29	243515	18.36	19	10.21	10
NC	4505372	15	300358	7.25	7	7.56	8
ND	322932	3	107644	1.16	1	1.75	2
OH	5580822	18	310046	9.12	9	8.58	9
OK	1334872	7	190696	2.33	2	4.67	5
OR	1789270	7	255610	3.80	4	2.95	3
PA	5753893	20	287695	10.39	11	9.32	9
RI	446049	4	111512	2.51	3	1.41	1
SC	1964118	9	218235	3.97	4	4.91	5
SD	363815	3	121272	1.20	1	1.74	2
TN	2458577	11	223507	4.30	4	6.54	7
TX	7993851	38	210365	15.73	16	21.72	22
UT	1019815	6	169969	1.48	1	4.36	5
VT	299290	3	99763	2.00	3	0.93	0
VA	3854489	13	296499	6.65	7	6.15	6
WA	3141106	12	261759	6.71	7	4.93	5
WV	670438	5	134088	1.78	2	3.11	3
WI	3071434	10	307143	5.28	5	4.59	5
WY	249061	3	83020	0.83	0	2.06	3
Totals		538		272.10	275	256.03	263
			Popular Vote Percentage	51.03%			47.19%
			Equal Voice Vote Percentage	51.12%			48.88%

The graphs on the following pages show the mix of Democratic and Republican activities within each state for the 2012 election. Rather than having each state weigh in as either a Democratic or Republican state, you'll see that there is a combination of each. Only Washington D.C. and Vermont were 100% vested in only one party for this election. Please note that the shadings used depict gray for Democrat and black for Republican.

Can you guess what the percentage was for your own state? I suggest you make a guess and then locate your state in the graphs below. You may be surprised at what you discover.

Equal Voice Voting

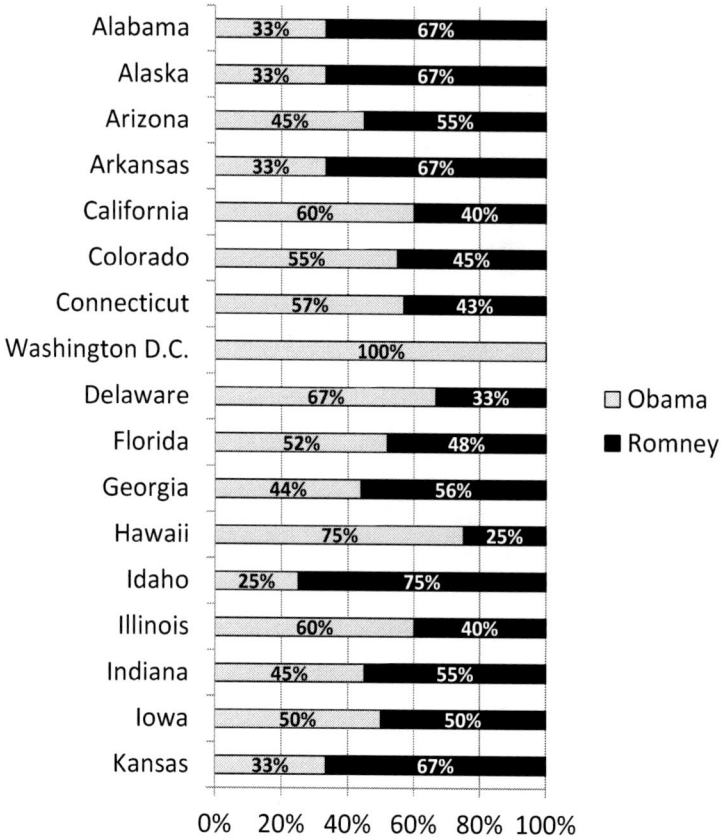

State	Obama	Romney
Alabama	33%	67%
Alaska	33%	67%
Arizona	45%	55%
Arkansas	33%	67%
California	60%	40%
Colorado	55%	45%
Connecticut	57%	43%
Washington D.C.	100%	
Delaware	67%	33%
Florida	52%	48%
Georgia	44%	56%
Hawaii	75%	25%
Idaho	25%	75%
Illinois	60%	40%
Indiana	45%	55%
Iowa	50%	50%
Kansas	33%	67%

0% 20% 40% 60% 80% 100%

☐ Obama
■ Romney

Figure 17: 2012 State Voting by Party Graph 1

Equal Voice Voting

The set of states shown here are rather balanced between the parties as are most of the states. Please remember that in each state, there are political voices that are silenced with our current voting system. The Equal Voice voting method would make those voices heard!

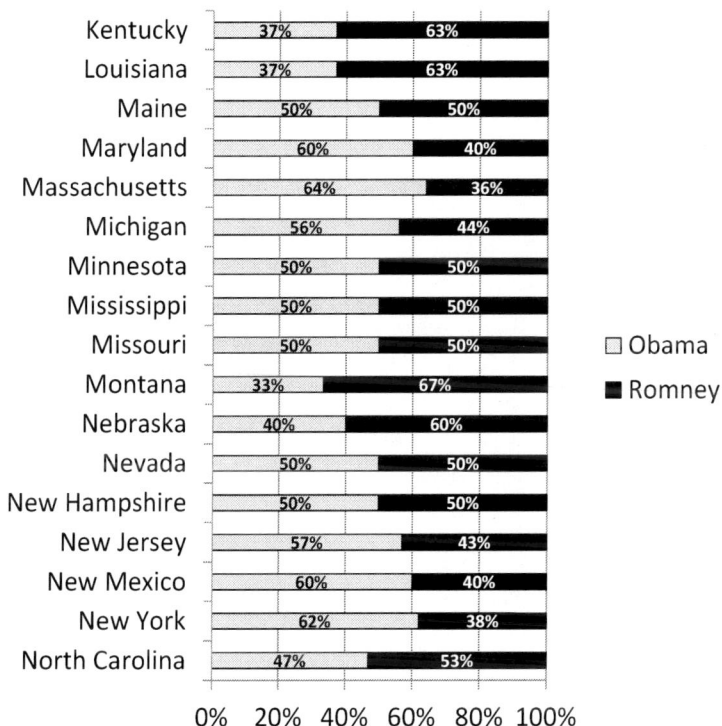

State	Obama	Romney
Kentucky	37%	63%
Louisiana	37%	63%
Maine	50%	50%
Maryland	60%	40%
Massachusetts	64%	36%
Michigan	56%	44%
Minnesota	50%	50%
Mississippi	50%	50%
Missouri	50%	50%
Montana	33%	67%
Nebraska	40%	60%
Nevada	50%	50%
New Hampshire	50%	50%
New Jersey	57%	43%
New Mexico	60%	40%
New York	62%	38%
North Carolina	47%	53%

Figure 18: 2012 State Voting by Party Graph 2

Using the current Electoral College method, Hawaii, Massachusetts, Nebraska, Oklahoma, Rhode Island, Utah, Vermont, and West Virginia experienced having every county being carried by only one party. If you looked at the voting results of those states from that perspective, it would appear that no opposing voice was significant in those respective states. Review those states (except Vermont) in these graphs and you'll quickly see that opposing voters in those states were not so silent! Though not shown for previous years, similar results would be experienced.

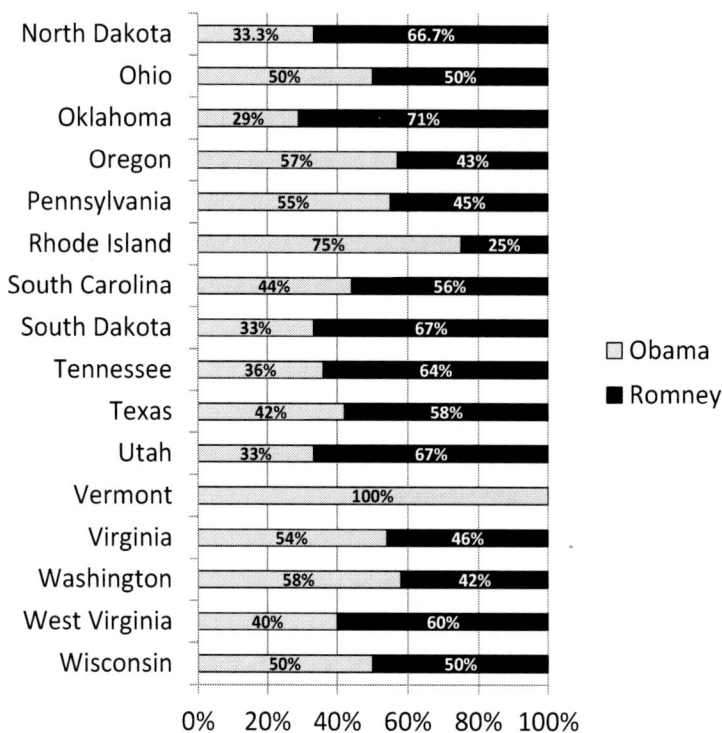

Figure 19: 2012 State Voting by Party Graph 3

Equal Voice Results – If Equal Voice Voting had been in place across our country in 2012, the election map would look like this.

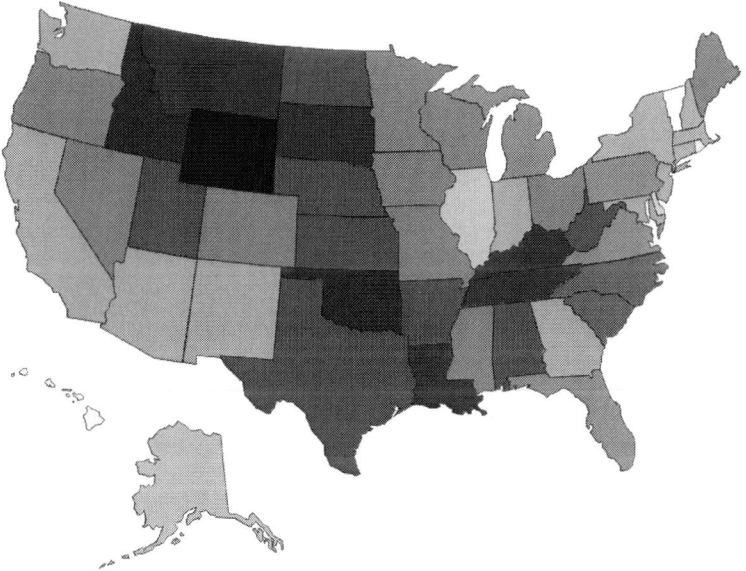

Figure 20: 2012 Equal Voice Voting Map

Two states and Washington D.C. (not depicted) are 100% for one party. Wyoming would have been 100% for Romney while Vermont and Washington D.C. would have been 100% for Obama. All others would be a mix, often close to a 50%/50% split, making the map shown above far more representative of those who voted than the one shown previously.

It is also the model depicted on this book's cover.

LET'S TALK

The key effort you can take to make a difference is to be part of the conversation. You've already taken the first step in that regard by reading this book. Now, I hope you will talk to others about it.

I encourage you to contact your state and federal representatives, any politically active organization, any political science study class, and any other interested group to further discuss these options. Please let your voice be heard – that you want our nation to elect its presidents in a more equitable manner than we have endured in the past.

We need to change how we exercise the Electoral College in this quest. The Equal Voice voting method provides a fairer representation of our citizens' voting intent. Our votes – our voices at the ballot box – need to represent our intent as we select our next president. Equal voting representation is a key hallmark of the democratic process.

The Equal Voice voting method does not require a constitutional amendment, nor even that every state adopts it at once. Your state can choose to enable the Equal Voice voting method as its Electoral College approach, giving the people in your state the voice and representation they deserve.

Your national representative to the House of Representatives can be located by visiting this website:

http://www.house.gov/

You can enter your zip code and then be linked to your representative's contact information.

Similarly, you can locate your state senators (every state has two) by logging into:

http://www.senate.gov/

You can locate your state and the contact information for your senators will appear.

Contact these people and let them know that you are interested in how our country votes. Mention that you've read this book and would like to be part of the discussion or at least weigh in with your supportive voice. Remember, every voice counts!

Appendix A – Popular Vote & Electoral College Results

Look at the solid bars in the graphs on the following pages and notice how they vary from each other. The gray bars represent the percentage of the popular votes won by the Democrats and the black bars show how much of the popular vote was won by the Republicans.

Notice how these solid bars (the popular votes) vary from each other (variance).In like manner, look at the striped bars. These represent the number of electoral votes a candidate received. The Democrat candidates are represented by the gray striped bars and the Republican candidates are represented by the black striped bars. Notice how much these bars vary from each other.

All of the presidential elections from 1980 through 2012 are included in the Appendix section. In elections that had third party contenders, those candidates gathered as much as 19% of the popular vote (1992) yet were never represented in the Electoral College in any of the four elections they were counted in the examples shown in the Appendix (1980, 1992, 1996, and 2000).

Notice how the popular votes for each candidate compare with the percentage of Electoral Votes.

Equal Voice Voting

2012 variances between the Democratic and Republican parties:

Popular Vote (solid bars) = 3.8%
Electoral Vote (striped bars) = 23.4%

2012

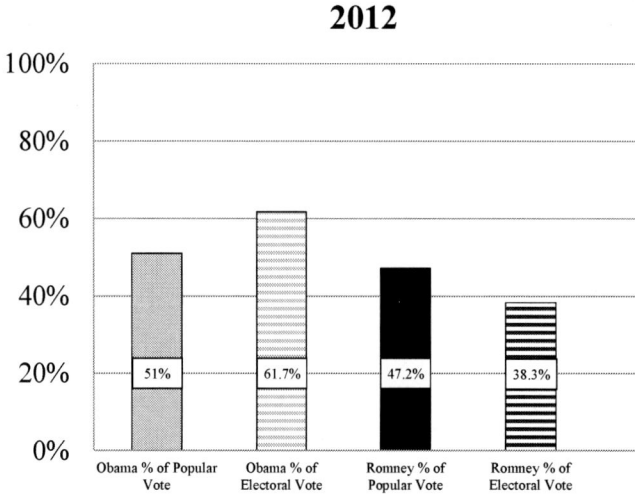

Figure 21: 2012 Popular & Electoral Voting Graph

2008 variances between the Democratic and Republican parties:

Popular Vote (solid bars) = 6.5%
Electoral Vote (striped bars) = 35.6%

2008

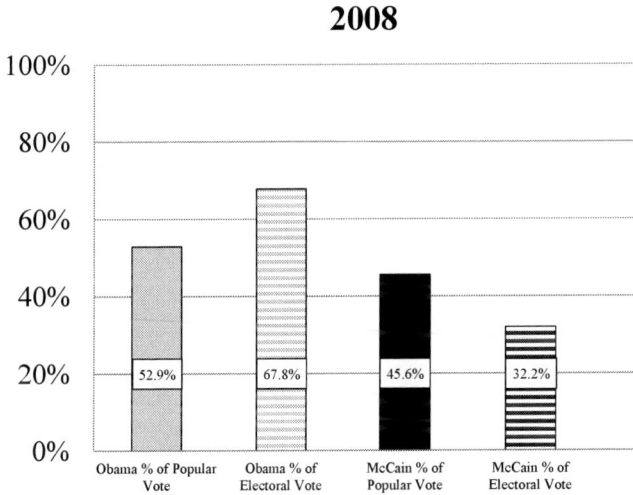

Figure 22: 2008 Popular & Electoral Voting Graph

2004 variances between the Democratic and Republican
parties:

Popular Vote (solid bars) = 2.4%
Electoral Vote (striped bars) = 6.4%

2004

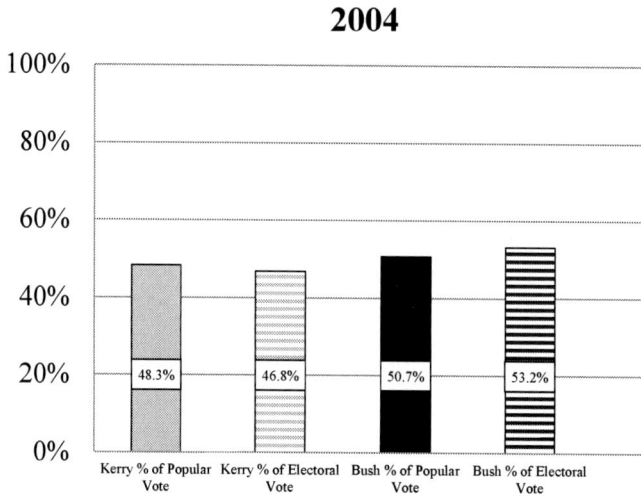

Figure 23: 2004 Popular & Electoral Voting Graph

Equal Voice Voting

2000 variances between the Democratic and Republican parties:

Popular Vote (solid bars) = 0.2%
Electoral Vote (striped bars) = 0.8%

2000

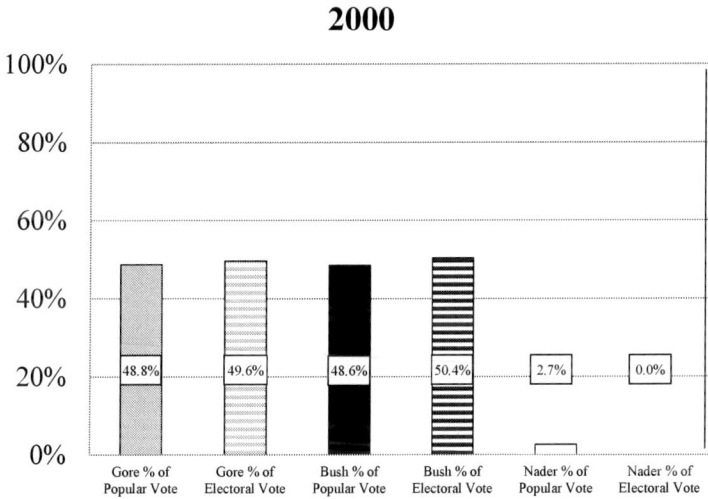

Figure 24: 2000 Popular & Electoral Voting Graph

Equal Voice Voting

1996 variances between the Democratic and Republican parties:

Popular Vote (solid bars) = 8.7%
Electoral Vote (striped bars) = 41%

1996

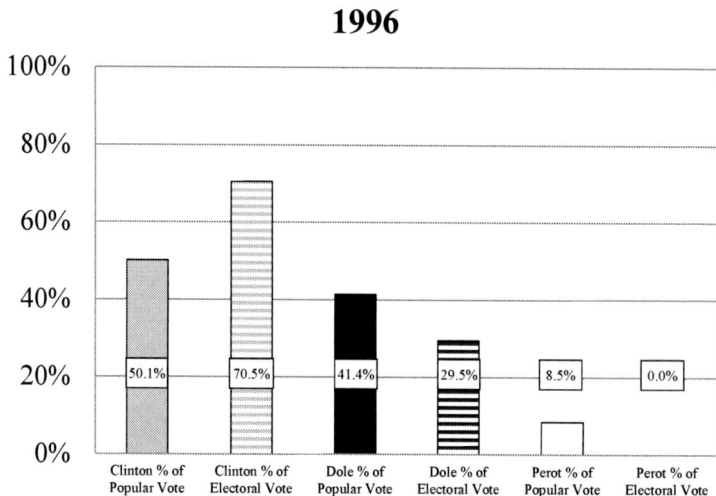

Figure 25: 1996 Popular & Electoral Voting Graph

1992 variances between the Democratic and Republican parties:

Popular Vote (solid bars) = 5.6%
Electoral Vote (striped bars) = 37.6%

1992

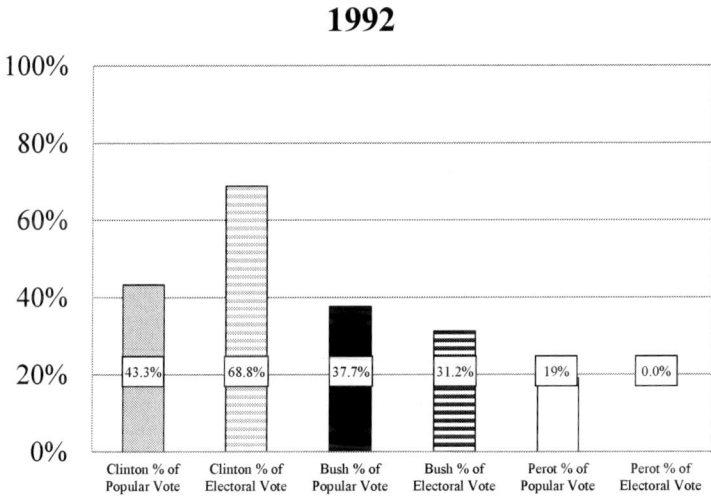

Figure 26: 1992 Popular & Electoral Voting Graph

1988 variances between the Democratic and Republican parties:

Popular Vote (solid bars) = 7.8%
Electoral Vote (striped bars) = 58.4%

1988

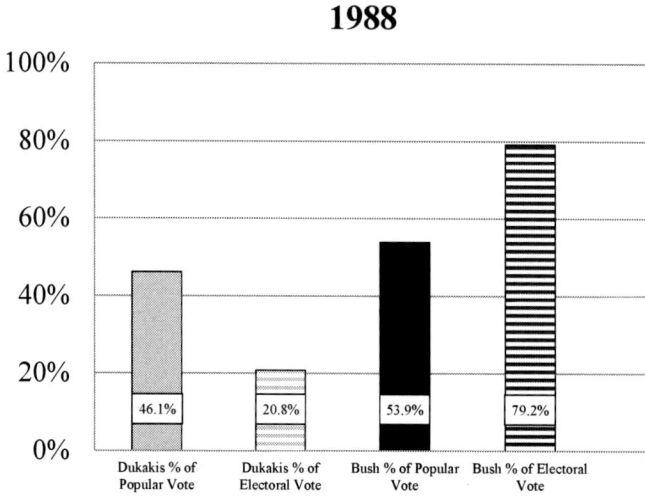

Figure 27: 1988 Popular & Electoral Voting Graph

1984 variances between the Democratic and Republican parties:

Popular Vote (solid bars) = 18.2%
Electoral Vote (striped bars) = 95.2%

1984

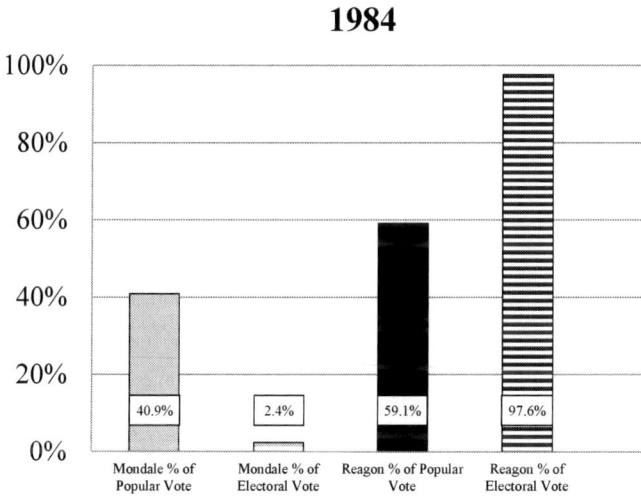

Figure 28: 1984 Popular & Electoral Voting Graph

1980 variances between the Democratic and Republican parties:

Popular Vote (solid bars) = 9.9%
Electoral Vote (striped bars) = 81.8%

1980

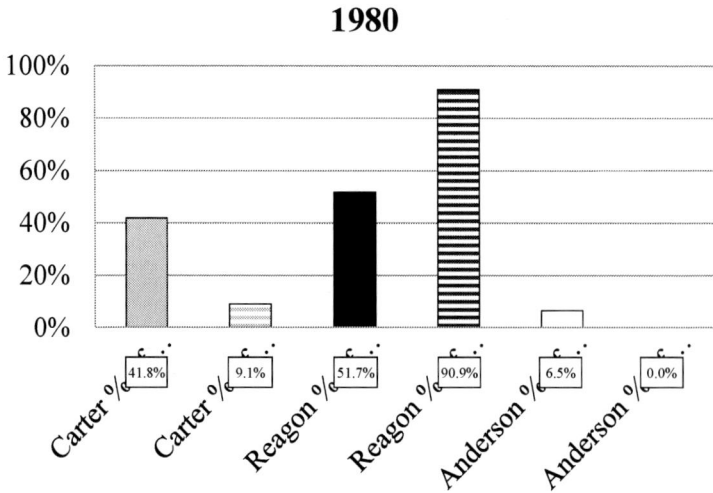

Figure 29: 1980 Popular & Electoral Voting Graph

APPENDIX B – CITY VOTING

Here are 50 cities depicted in five different graphs, each showing the percentage of votes gained by either Obama (in gray) or Romney (in black) during the 2012 election. Notice that the winning party for the state is identified with either a capital "D" or "R" (Democrat or Republican), respectively.

Note: Exact city voting was not captured for this display. Rather, the key county each city is in is presented here.

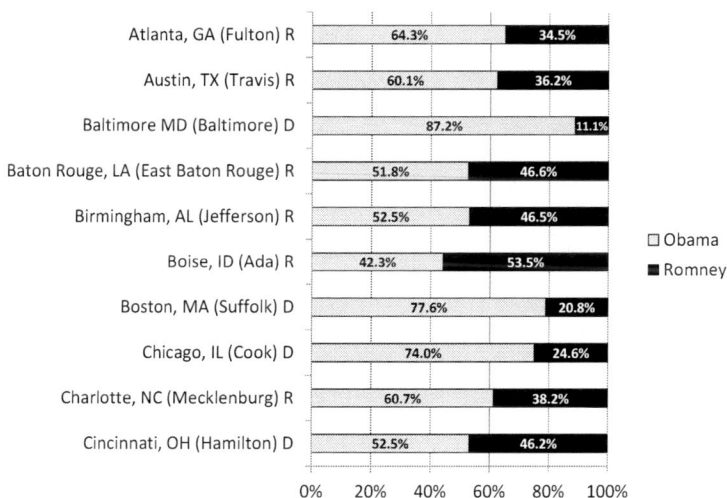

Figure 30: 2012 City Voting Graph 1

Baltimore, Boston, Chicago, and Cincinnati are in states which were won by Obama. The other cities are in states that were won by Romney.

Atlanta, Austin, Baton Rouge, Birmingham, and Charlotte had a majority of their voters selecting the candidate that did not win the state!

Equal Voice Voting

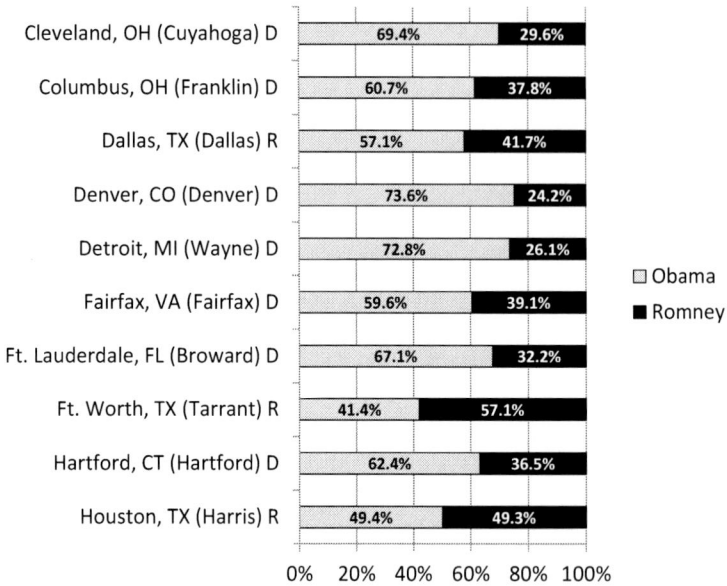

Figure 31: 2012 City Voting Graph 2

Dallas, Ft. Worth, and Houston are in states that were won by Romney. The other cities are in states that were won by Obama. Notice how close the voting was in Houston! This is the closest voting of any of the 50 depicted in these graphs.

Dallas is the only city of these ten that had a majority of its voters selecting the candidate that did not win the state!

Equal Voice Voting

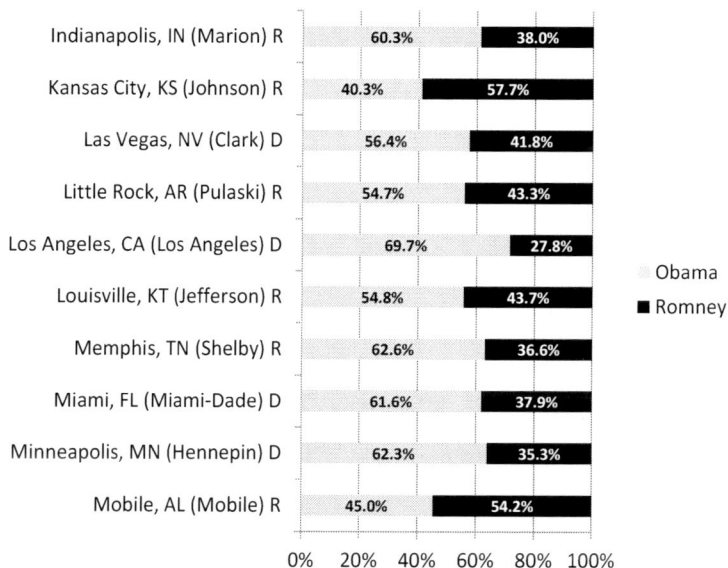

City	Obama	Romney
Indianapolis, IN (Marion) R	60.3%	38.0%
Kansas City, KS (Johnson) R	40.3%	57.7%
Las Vegas, NV (Clark) D	56.4%	41.8%
Little Rock, AR (Pulaski) R	54.7%	43.3%
Los Angeles, CA (Los Angeles) D	69.7%	27.8%
Louisville, KT (Jefferson) R	54.8%	43.7%
Memphis, TN (Shelby) R	62.6%	36.6%
Miami, FL (Miami-Dade) D	61.6%	37.9%
Minneapolis, MN (Hennepin) D	62.3%	35.3%
Mobile, AL (Mobile) R	45.0%	54.2%

0%   20%   40%   60%   80%   100%

Figure 32: 2012 City Voting Graph 3

Las Vegas, Los Angeles, Miami, and Minneapolis are in states that were won by Obama. The other cities are in states that were won by Romney.

Indianapolis, Little Rock, Louisville, and Memphis had a majority of their voters selecting the candidate that did not win the state!

Equal Voice Voting

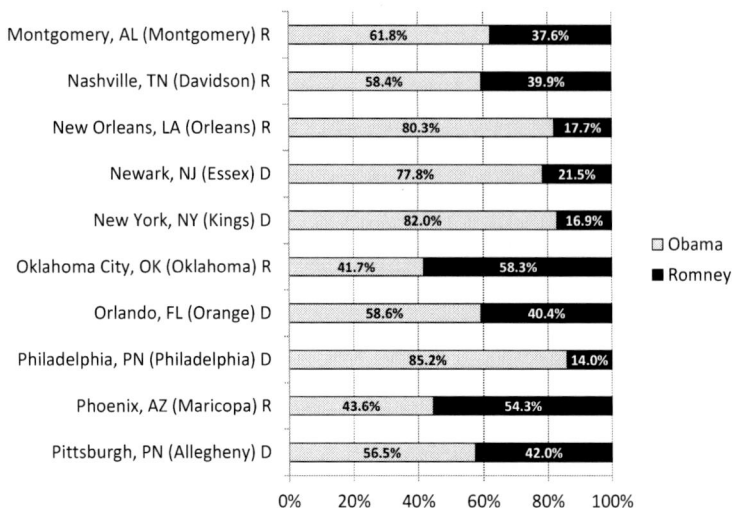

Figure 33: 2012 City Voting Graph 4

Half of these cities are in states won by Obama and the other half in states won by Romney. Newark, New York, Orlando, Philadelphia, and Pittsburgh are in states that were won by Obama. The other cities are in states that were won by Romney.

Montgomery, Nashville, and New Orleans had a majority of their voters selecting the candidate that did not win the state! New Orleans had the largest percentage of its population voting for the losing candidate of its state of any depicted in these 50 cities.

Equal Voice Voting

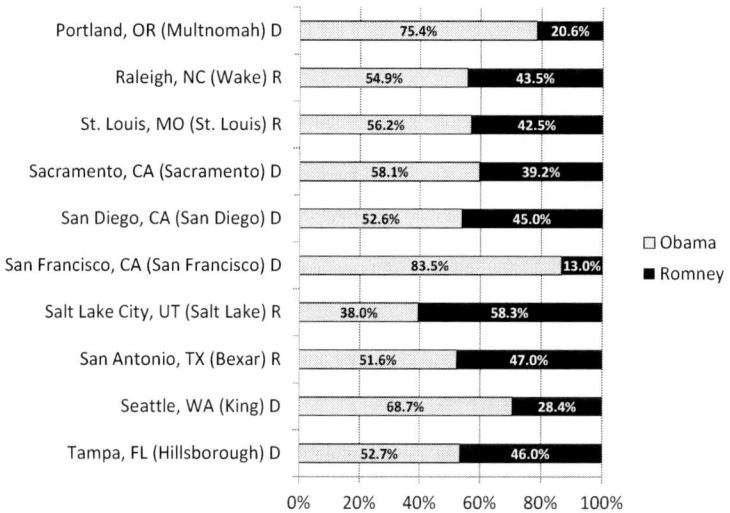

Figure 34: 2012 City Voting Graph 5

Raleigh, St. Louis, Salt Lake City, and San Antonio are in states that were won by Romney. The other cities are in states that were won by Obama. San Francisco is the city of these 50 that shows the highest percentage of voters casting their ballot for the state winning candidate. Philadelphia, New York, and New Orleans were also cities with voting populations that were most lopsided in their voting.

Equal Voice Voting

Page B-6

APPENDIX C – GERRYMANDERED DISTRICTS

The following 20 pages show congressional districts that have been subjected to gerrymandering. Ten of them are currently held by Democrats and ten by Republicans. The maps are taken from the www.NationalAtlas.gov website. Notice how convoluted they are (salamanders?) as they strive to include the party of choice voters and exclude others. Words like *Control, Manipulation*, and *Unfair* should spring to mind.

Alabama's 6th Congressional District is currently held by Republicans.

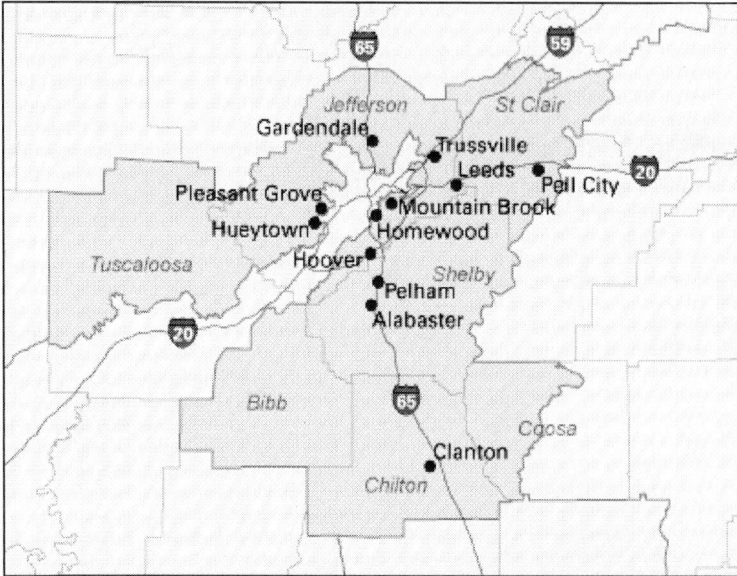

Figure 35: Alabama Congressional District #6

Alabama's 7th Congressional District is currently held by Democrats.

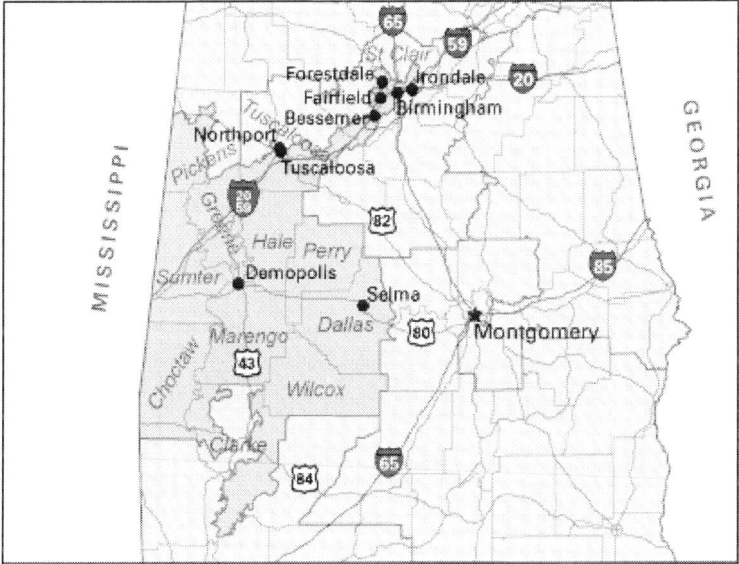

Figure 35: Alabama Congressional District #7

California's 18ᵗʰ Congressional District is currently held by Democrats.

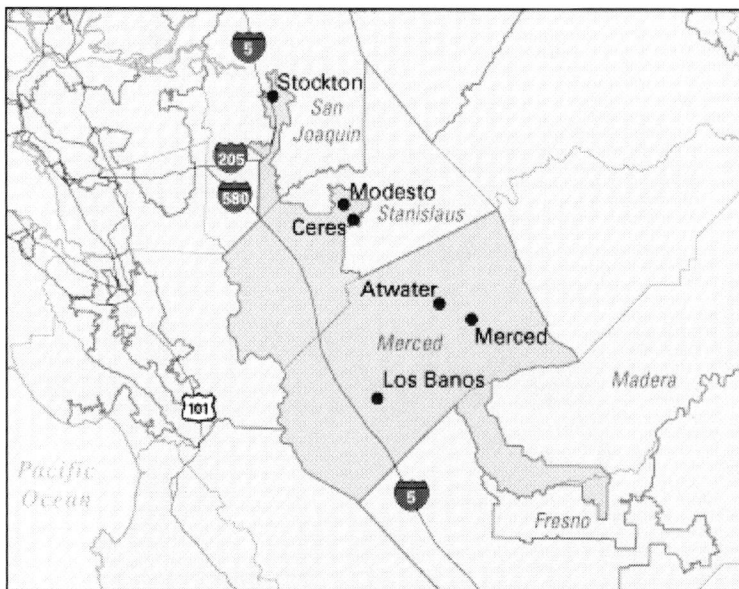

Figure 36: California Congressional District #18

California's 44th Congressional District is currently held by Republicans.

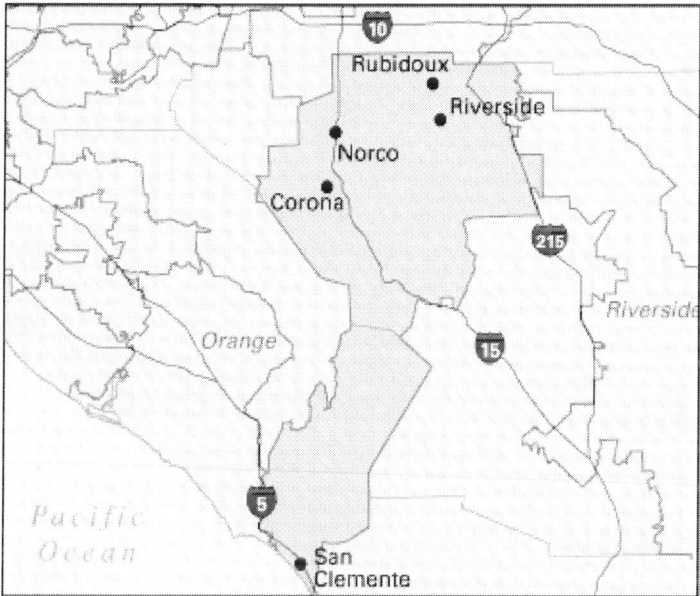

Figure 37: California Congressional District #44

Connecticut's 1st Congressional District is currently held by Democrats.

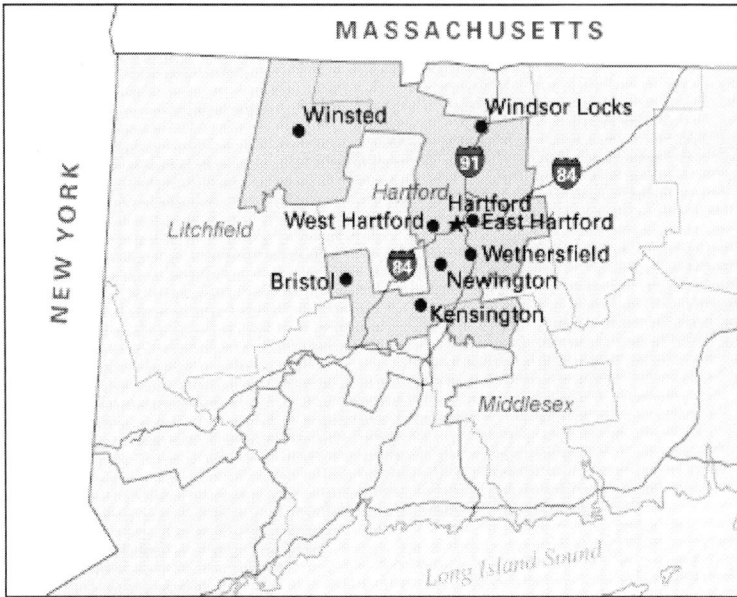

Figure 38: Connecticut Congressional District #1

Florida's 3rd Congressional District is held by Democrats.

Figure 39: Florida Congressional District #3

Florida's 8th Congressional District is held by
Republicans.

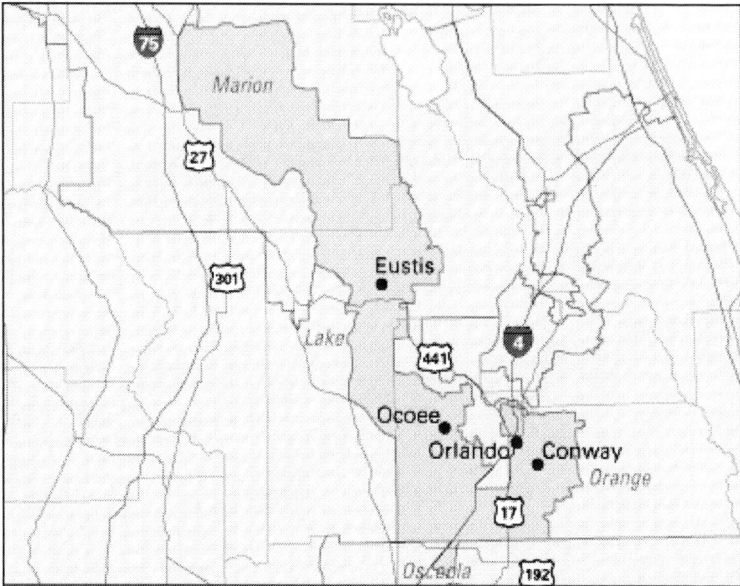

Figure 40: Florida Congressional District #8

Florida's 9th Congressional District is held by
Republicans.

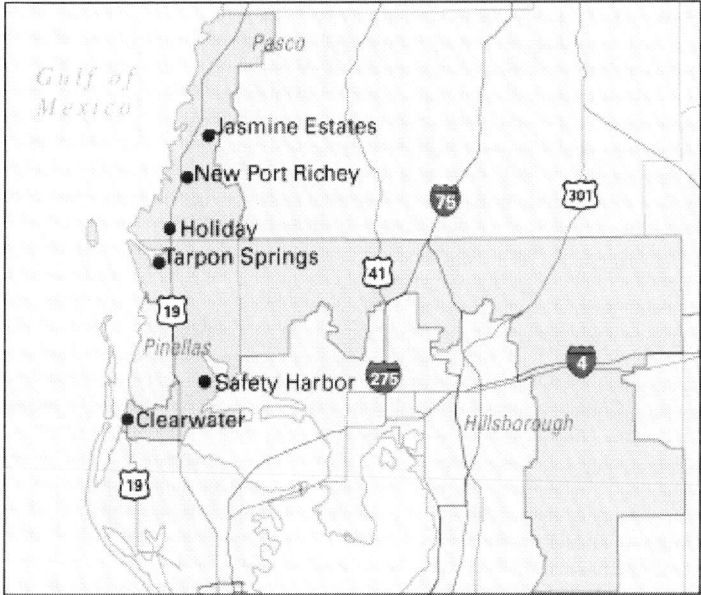

Figure 41: Florida Congressional District #9

Georgia's 13th Congressional District is currently held by Democrats.

Figure 42: Georgia Congressional District #13

Illinois's 17th Congressional District is held by Republicans.

Figure 43: Illinois Congressional District #17

Maryland's 2nd Congressional District is currently held by Democrats.

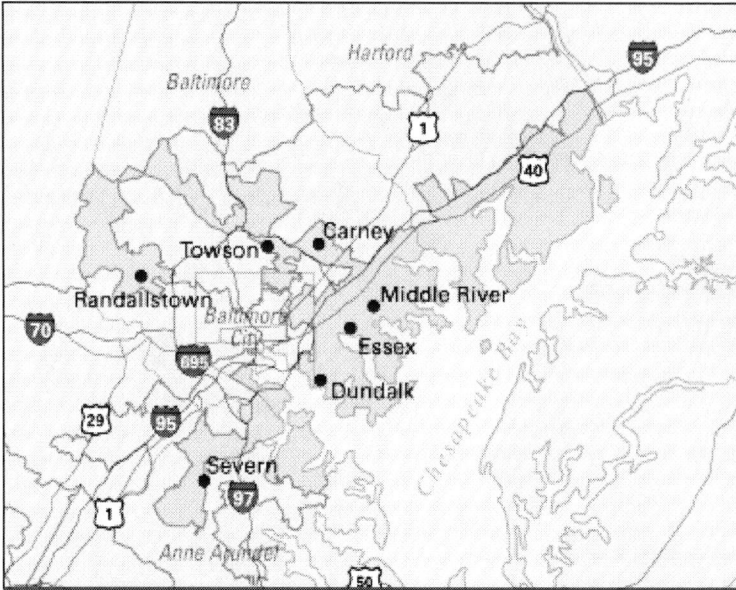

Figure 44: Maryland Congressional District #2

Maryland's 3rd Congressional District is currently held by Democrats.

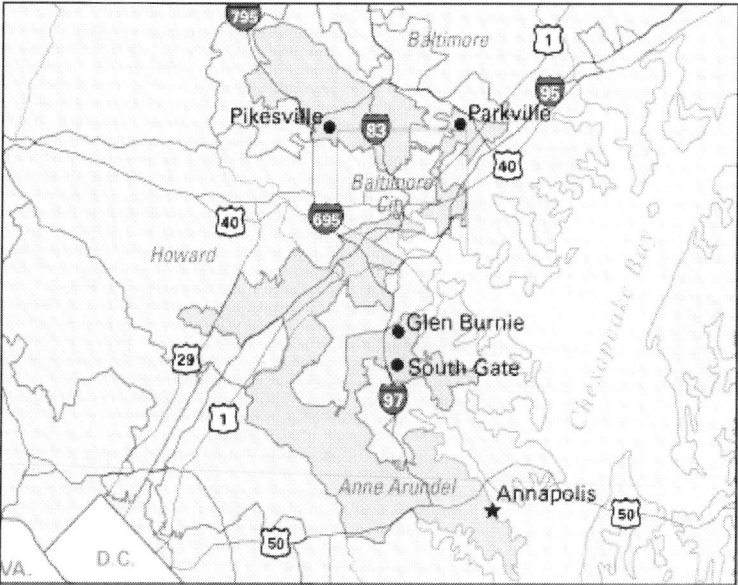

Figure 45: Maryland Congressional District #3

Massachusetts' 4th Congressional District is currently held by Democrats.

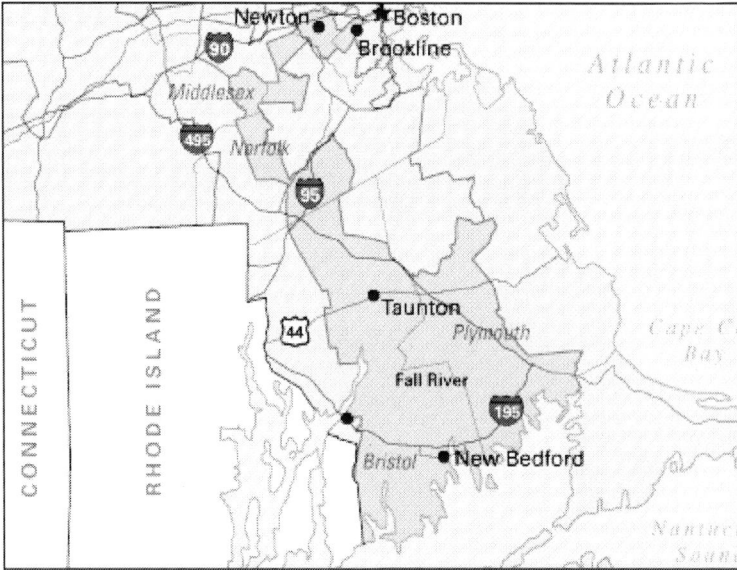

Figure 46: Massachusetts Congressional District #4

New Jersey's 6th Congressional District is currently held by Democrats.

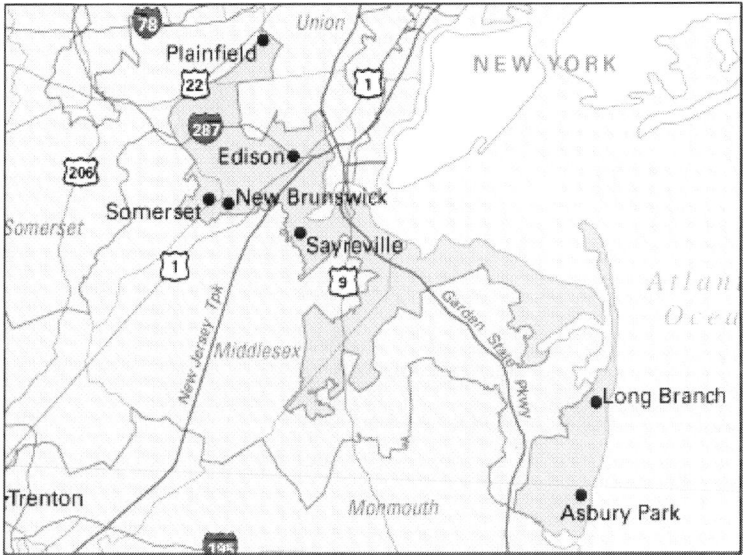

Figure 47: New Jersey Congressional District #6

New York's 24th Congressional District is currently held by Republicans.

Figure 48: New York Congressional District #24

North Carolina's 12th Congressional District is currently held by Democrats.

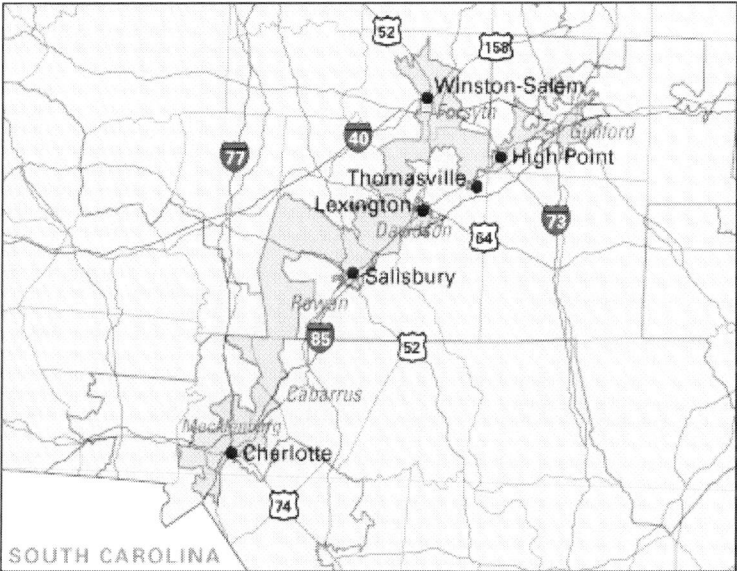

Figure 49: North Carolina Congressional District #12

Ohio's 18th Congressional District is currently held by Republicans.

Figure 50: Ohio Congressional District #18

Pennsylvania's 18th Congressional District is currently held by Republicans.

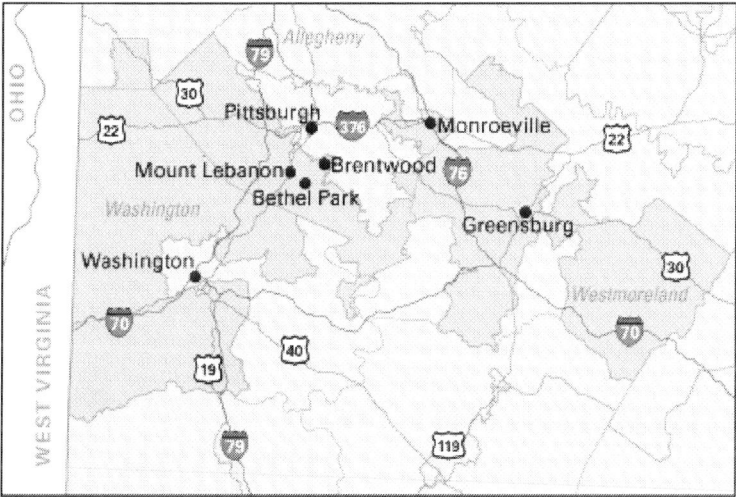

Figure 51: Pennsylvania Congressional District #18

South Carolina's 2nd Congressional District is currently held by Republicans.

Figure 52: South Carolina Congressional District #2

Tennessee's 3rd Congressional District is currently held by Republicans.

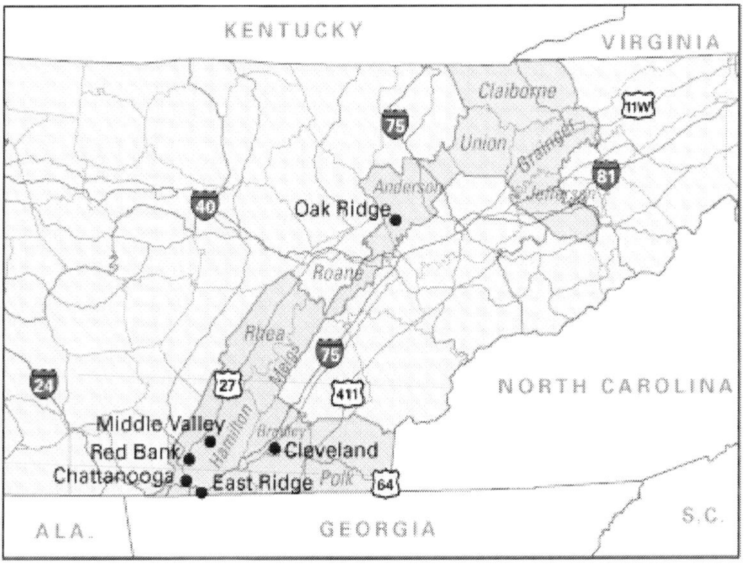

Figure 53: Tennessee Congressional District #3

Equal Voice Voting

APPENDIX D – EQUAL VOICE VOTING RESULTS

The following graphs are shown here to compare the nine example elections (1980 – 2012) between the popular votes, electoral votes cast, and how these same elections would fare under the Equal Voice voting method. The gray bars depict the results for the Democrats; the black bars depict the results for the Republicans. Some graphs use black bars for 3rd party candidates, when needed.

As you review the charts, notice how close in height the popular votes (solid bars) compare to the Equal Voice Votes (vertical striped bars). Then compare these heights with the Electoral College results depicted here with the horizontal striped bars. Typically, these bars vary significantly from the other two.

Equal Voice Voting

The 2012 election shows that Obama won by a large margin when considering the Electoral College votes. Yet, his victory was only won by a 3.8% popular vote margin. The EVVs won by both candidates clearly shows a more equal representation.

2012

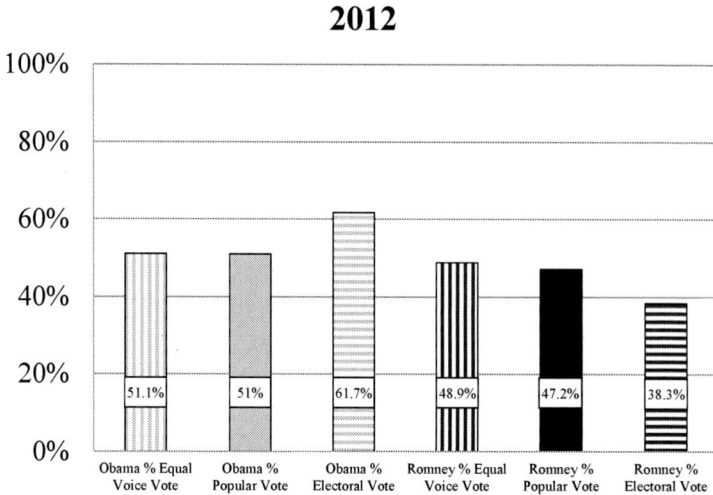

Figure 54: 2012 EV, Popular & Electoral Vote Graph

Variances between parties:

Popular Votes (solid bars) =
    51%:47.2% = 3.8%
Electoral Votes (horizontal striped bars) =
    61.7%:38.3% = 23.4%
EVVs (vertical striped bars) = 51.1%:48.9% = 2.2%
Variance between EVVs and Popular Votes:
    Democrat = 51.1%:51% = 0.1%
    Republican = 48.9%:47.2% = 1.7%

Obama won 53.7% of the EVVs compared to 46.3% won by McCain (only a 7.4% variance). Yet the Electoral College voting shows that Obama gained twice the electoral votes as did McCain.

2008

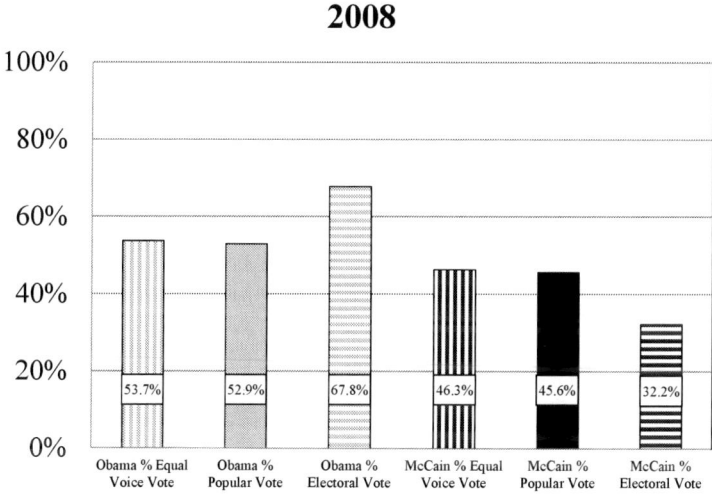

Figure 55: 2008 EV, Popular & Electoral Vote Graph

Variances between parties:

Popular Votes (solid bars) =
    52.9%:45.6% = 7.3%
Electoral Votes (horizontal striped bars) =
    67.8%:32.2% = 35.6%
EVVs (vertical striped bars) = 53.7%:46.3% = 7.4%
Variance between EVVs and Popular Votes:
    Democrat = 53.7%:52.9% = 0.8%
    Republican = 46.3%:45.6% = 0.7%

2000, 2004 and 2012 are the closest races in terms of
variances between the popular votes and their respective
Electoral College results. As you see here, all six bars range
between the 40% and 60% marks. It simply means that
number of states won and their respective electoral vote
totals were divided more equally between the candidates
than the other six elections.

2004

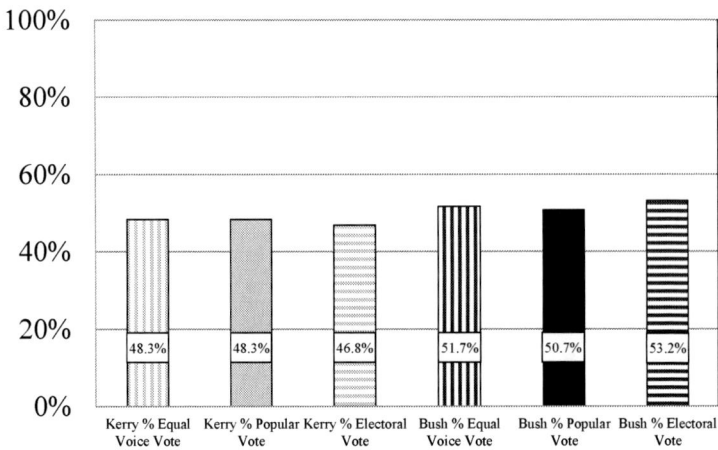

Figure 56: 2004 EV, Popular & Electoral Vote Graph

Variances between parties:

Popular Votes (solid bars) =
48.3%:50.7% = 2.4%
Electoral Votes (horizontal striped bars) =
46.8%:53.2% = 6.4%
EVVs (vertical striped bars) = 48.3%:51.7% = 3.4%
Variance between EVVs and Popular Votes:
Democrat = 48.3%:48.3% = 0%
Republican = 51.7%:50.7% = 1%

Equal Voice Voting

The most contentious race of the nine examples shows that the winning candidate won the popular vote by only 0.2%, the closest popular vote variance of any example shown here. The electoral votes were similarly close, having only a 0.8% difference. However, **Gore won the election by only one EV vote!** Interestingly, an examination of the data shows that a few hundred votes made the difference in New Mexico! (See the Election Stories for 2000.)

2000

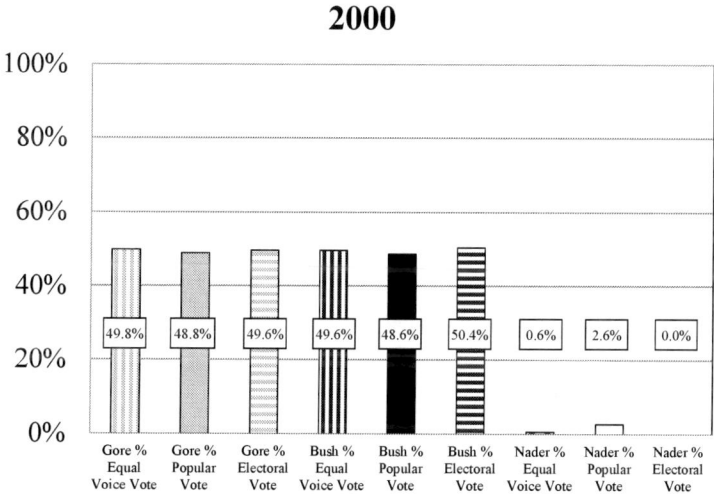

Figure 57: 2000 EV, Popular & Electoral Vote Graph

Variances between parties:
Popular Votes (solid bars) =
    48.8%:48.6% = 0.2%
Electoral Votes (horizontal striped bars) =
    49.6%:50.4% = 0.8%
EVVs (vertical striped bars) = 49.8%:49.6% = 0.2%
Variance between EVVs and Popular Votes:
    Democrat = 49.8%:49.8% = 0%
    Republican = 49.6%:48.6% = 1%

Similar to the race in 1992, this election was within an 8.7% margin in terms of the popular vote. Yet the electoral votes were far more than double for Clinton as compared to those gained by Dole. Again, Perot earned no electoral votes but would have realized at least a 4.8% representation with the EV voting method.

1996

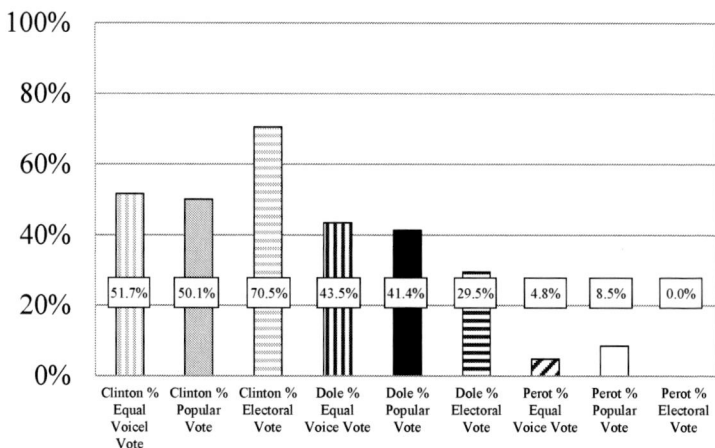

Figure 58: 1996 EV, Popular & Electoral Vote Graph

Variances between parties:

Popular Votes (solid bars) =
    50.1%:41.4% = 8.7%
Electoral Votes (horizontal striped bars) =
    70.5%:29.5% = 41%
EVVs (vertical striped bars) = 51.7%:43.5% = 8.2%
Variance between EVVs and Popular Votes:
    Democrat = 51.7%:50.1% = 1.6%
    Republican = 43.5%:41.4% = 2.1%

There was only a 5.6% popular vote difference between the Democratic and Republican candidates yet Clinton gained more than twice as many electoral votes as did Bush.

Notice how Perot captured almost 20% of the popular vote yet earned no electoral votes. Using the EV voting method, Perot would have captured 15.6% of the EVVs.

1992

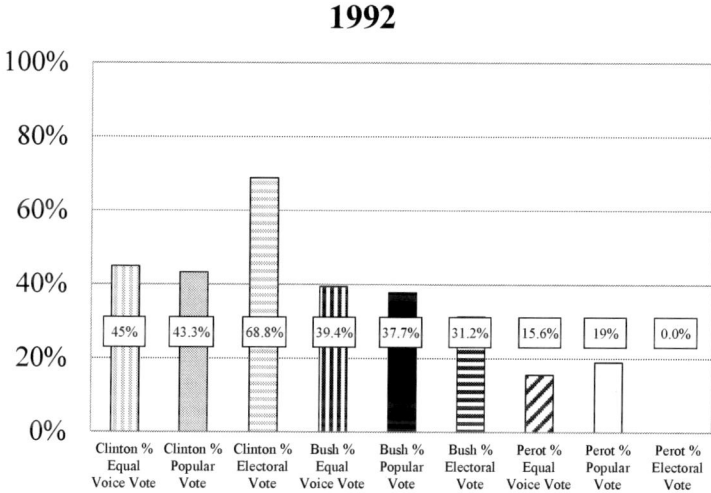

Figure 59: 1992 EV, Popular & Electoral Vote Graph

Variances between parties:

Popular Votes (solid bars) =
    43.3%:37.7% = 5.6%
Electoral Votes (horizontal striped bars) =
    68.8%:31.2% = 37.6%
EVVs (vertical striped bars) = 45%:39.4% = 6.1%
Variance between EVVs and Popular Votes:
    Democrat = 45%:43.3% = 1.7%
    Republican = 39.4%:37.7% = 1.7%

Equal Voice Voting

The Republican candidate collected almost four times as many electoral votes as did the Democratic candidate, though the popular vote was only 15% greater. Notice that the EVVs and popular vote variances are only 0.2% for both parties!

1988

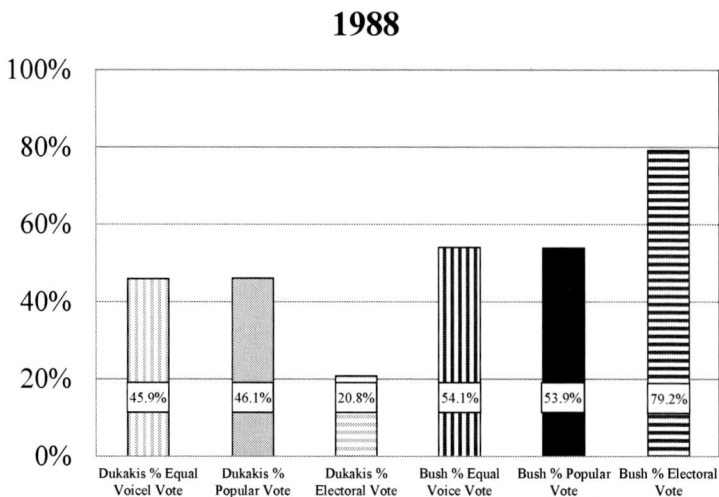

Figure 60: 1988 EV, Popular & Electoral Vote Graph

Variances between parties:

Popular Votes (solid bars) =
  46.1%:53.9% = 7.8%
Electoral Votes (horizontal striped bars) =
  20.8%:79.2% = 58.4%
EVVs (vertical striped bars) = 45.9%:54.1% = 8.2%
Variance between EVVs and Popular Votes:
  Democrat = 45.9%:46.1% = 0.2%
  Republican = 54.1%:53.9% = 0.2%

This graph shows the highest number of electoral votes cast for one candidate of the nine examples shown. 95.2% more electoral votes were cast for the winner though there was less than 20% popular vote difference between the candidates.

1984

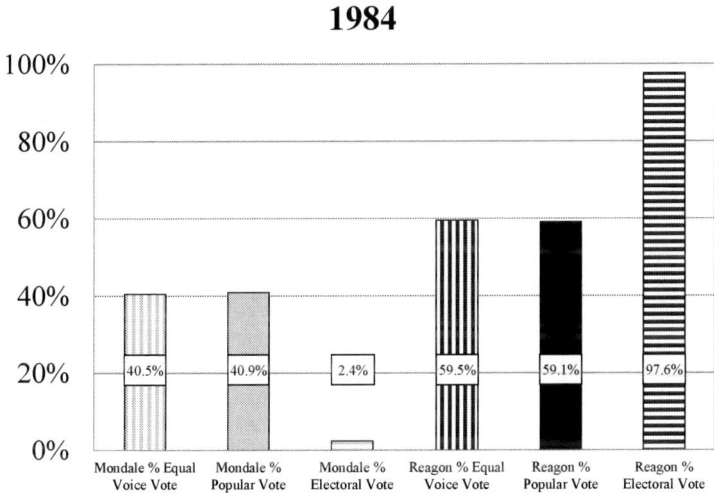

Figure 61: 1984 EV, Popular & Electoral Vote Graph

Variances between parties:

Popular Votes (solid bars) =
    40.9%:59.1% = 19.8%
Electoral Votes (horizontal striped bars) =
    2.4%:97.6% = 95.2%
EVVs (vertical striped bars) = 40.5%:59.5% = 19%
Variance between EVVs and Popular Votes:
    Democrat = 40.5%:40.9% = 0.4%
    Republican = 59.5%:59.1% = 0.4%

Equal Voice Voting

This graph for the 1980 election shows the second highest number of electoral votes (Republican 90.9%) cast for one candidate of the nine examples shown. Yet there was only a 9.9% variance between the two candidates for the popular vote.

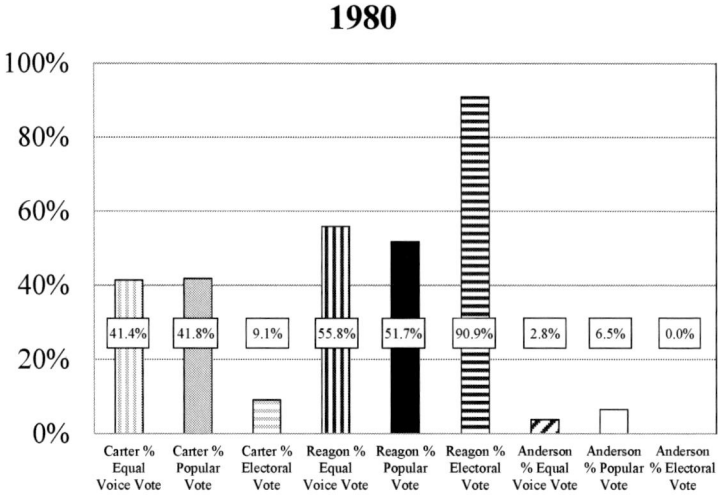

Figure 62: 1980 EV, Popular & Electoral Vote Graph

Variances between parties:

Popular Votes (solid bars) =
    41.8%:51.7% = 9.9%
Electoral Votes (horizontal striped bars) =
    9.1%:90.9% = 81.8%
EVVs (vertical striped bars) = 41.4%:55.8% = 14.4%
Variance between EVVs and Popular Votes:
    Democrat = 41.4%:41.8% = 0.4%
    Republican = 55.8%:51.7% = 4.1%

Page D-10

APPENDIX E – MAPS & DATA OF PAST ELECTIONS

Depictions of our United States and tables are provided below to further illustrate how the EV voting method could have made a difference in the past nine elections (1980 – 2012). You may wish to compare your own state with those that border yours, or where your friends and relatives live. Notice how different elections show different representations.

Equal Voice Voting

2008 Presidential Election

Look at the map: The map of the electoral vote state wins below appears balanced (McCain winning 22 states, Obama 28 states and Washington D.C.). The map reveals the balance actually tips towards McCain, if you consider the land area involved. However, Obama won by a 36% margin (365 electoral votes vs. 173 for McCain), using the current Electoral College voting method.

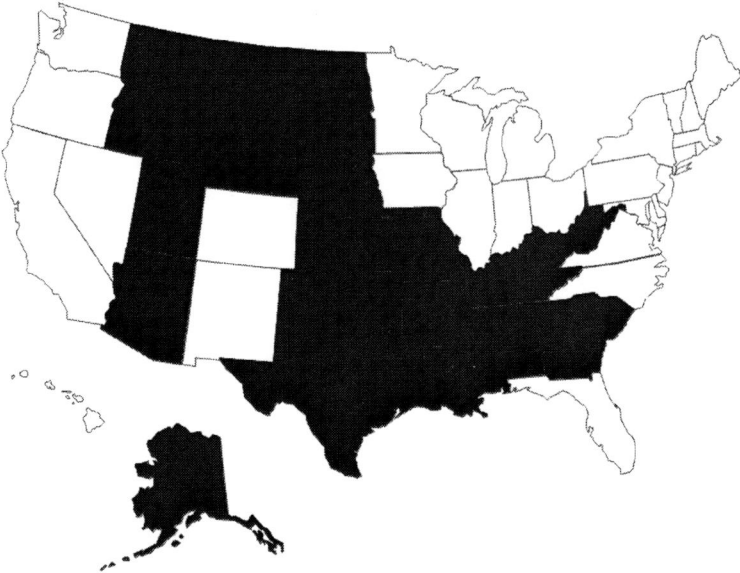

Figure 63: 2008 Electoral Vote Map

Things to consider: The electoral vote margin won by the Democrat candidate (Obama) was greater than a two to one victory over the Republican candidate (McCain) in 2008. Yet, if the EV voting method had been used, Obama's electoral vote victory would have been reduced to 40 votes, which is only 7.44%. 12 states tied in the number of Equal Voice Votes (EVVs).

Using the current Electoral College method, Connecticut, Hawaii, Massachusetts, Rhode Island, and Vermont experienced having every county being carried by only one party. Using the EV voting method, the voting voice of those states are split by the following percentages showing many voter votes in these states were not represented.

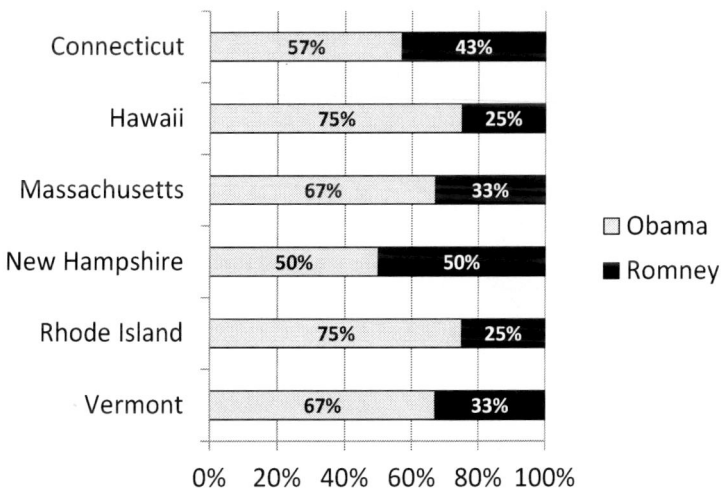

Figure 64: 2008 Selected State Voting Graph

Four states (highlighted in gray in the next table) tied in the number of EVVs. Only Washington D.C. (highlighted in black in the next table) awarded all of its EVVs to one candidate.

Table 13: 2008 Example Election Results

States	Popular Vote	Electoral Votes	PVV	Obama	Obama EVVs	McCain	McCain EVVs
AL	2,099,819	9	233,313	3.49	3	5.43	6
AK	326,197	3	108,732	1.14	1	1.78	2
AZ	2,303,838	10	230,384	4.49	4	5.34	6
AR	1,086,617	6	181,103	2.33	2	3.52	4
CA	13,577,265	55	246,859	33.52	35	20.30	20
CO	2,401,462	9	266,829	4.83	5	4.02	4
CT	1,646,793	7	235,256	4.24	4	2.68	3
DE	412,616	3	137,539	1.86	2	1.11	1
DC	265,853	3	88,618	2.77	3	0.20	0
FL	8,411,861	27	311,550	13.75	14	12.99	13
GA	3,932,158	15	262,144	7.03	7	7.82	8
HI	453,568	4	113,392	2.87	3	1.06	1
ID	658,454	4	164,614	1.44	1	2.45	3
IL	5,528,499	21	263,262	12.99	13	7.72	8
IN	2,756,340	11	250,576	5.48	6	5.37	5
IA	1,537,123	7	219,589	3.77	4	3.11	3
KS	1,238,873	6	206,479	2.49	2	3.39	4
KY	1,827,587	8	228,448	3.29	3	4.59	5
LA	1,960,761	9	217,862	3.59	4	5.27	5
ME	731,163	4	182,791	2.31	2	1.62	2
MD	2,631,596	10	263,160	6.19	6	3.65	4
MA	3,081,069	12	256,756	7.42	8	4.32	4
MI	5,010,299	17	294,723	9.75	10	6.95	7
MN	2,910,369	10	291,037	5.41	6	4.38	4
MS	1,289,939	6	214,990	2.58	3	3.37	3
MO	2,929,111	11	266,283	5.41	5	5.43	6
MT	492,750	3	164,250	1.41	1	1.48	2
NE	801,281	5	160,256	2.08	2	2.83	3
NV	967,848	5	193,570	2.76	3	2.13	2
NH	710,970	4	177,743	2.17	2	1.78	2
NJ	3,877,407	15	258,494	8.57	9	6.24	6
NM	830,158	6	166,032	2.85	3	2.09	2
NY	7,640,948	31	246,482	19.49	20	11.17	11
NC	4,310,789	15	287,386	7.46	8	7.41	7
ND	317,738	3	105,913	1.34	1	1.59	2
OH	5,721,815	20	286,091	10.28	11	9.36	9
OK	1,462,661	7	208,952	2.40	2	4.60	5
OR	1,827,864	7	261,123	3.97	4	2.83	3
PA	6,015,476	21	286,451	11.44	12	9.27	9
RI	471,766	4	117,942	2.51	3	1.40	1
SC	1,920,969	8	240,121	3.59	4	4.31	4
SD	381,975	3	127,325	1.34	1	1.59	2
TN	2,601,982	11	236,544	4.60	5	6.25	6
TX	8,087,402	34	237,865	14.83	15	18.83	19
UT	957,590	5	191,518	1.71	2	3.11	3
VT	325,046	3	108,349	2.02	2	0.91	1
VA	3,723,260	13	286,405	6.84	7	6.02	6
WA	3,053,254	11	277,569	6.31	7	4.43	4
WV	714,868	5	142,974	2.13	2	2.78	3
WI	2,983,417	10	298,342	5.62	6	4.23	4
WY	254,658	3	84,886	0.98	1	1.94	2
Totals		538		283	289	246	249
			Popular Vote Percentage	52.87%		45.60%	
			Equal Voice Vote Percentage	53.72%		46.28%	

2004 Presidential Election

Look at the map: Kerry's electoral voting margin was about 6% less than Bush's (Bush winning 286 electoral votes to Kerry's 251). Still, the map below appears to be overwhelmingly in favor of Bush, suggesting that the margin should be much greater if it were to accurately reflect the voting results.

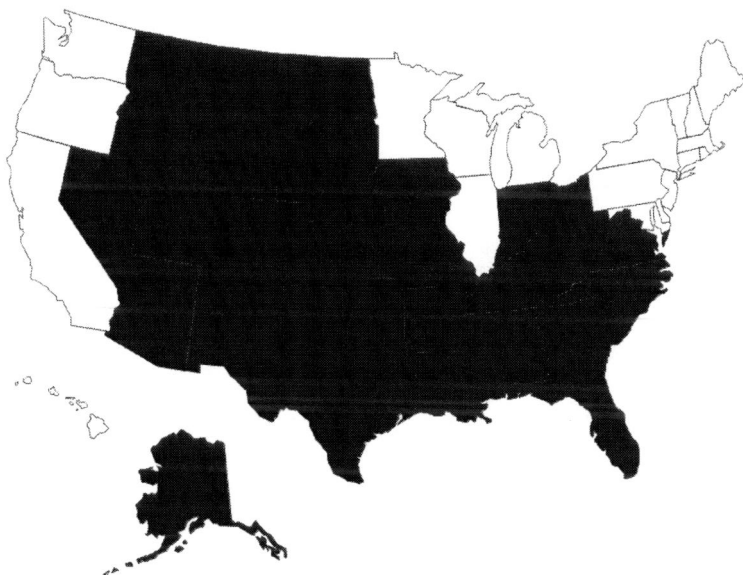

Figure 65: 2004 Electoral Vote Map

Things to consider: If the EV voting method had been used, the Republican margin of victory would have been 3.34%. The results are hidden, if you only review the map, as it does not reflect the votes captured. Remember, ten states evenly split their EV votes with the remaining states remaining less polarized than what the map above indicates. ten states tied in the number of Equal Voice Votes (EVVs).

Equal Voice Voting

Using the current Electoral College method, Hawaii, Massachusetts, and Rhode Island experienced having every county being carried by only one party. Using the EV voting method, the voting voice of those states are split by the following percentages showing many votes in these states were not represented:

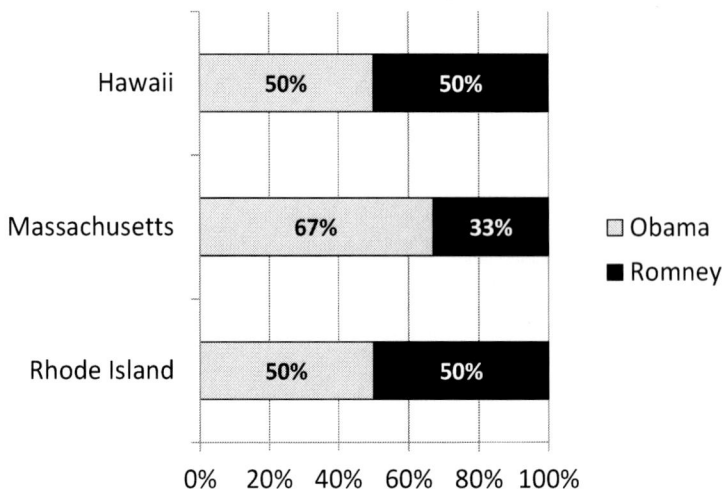

Figure 66: 2004 Selected State Voting Graph

Ten states (highlighted in gray in the next table) tied in the number of EVVs. Only Washington D.C. (highlighted in black in the next table) awarded all of its EVVs to one candidate.

Equal Voice Voting
Table 14: 2004 Example Election Results

States	Popular Vote	Electoral Votes	PVV	Kerry	Kerry EVVs	Bush	Bush EVVs
AL	1,883,449	9	209,272	3.32	3	5.62	6
AK	312,598	3	104,199	1.07	1	1.83	2
AZ	2,012,585	10	201,259	4.44	4	5.49	6
AR	1,054,945	6	175,824	2.67	3	3.26	3
CA	12,419,857	55	225,816	29.87	31	24.40	24
CO	2,130,330	9	236,703	4.23	4	4.65	5
CT	1,578,769	7	225,538	3.80	4	3.08	3
DE	375,190	3	125,063	1.60	2	1.37	1
DC	227,586	3	75,862	2.68	3	0.28	0
FL	7,609,810	27	281,845	12.71	13	14.07	14
GA	3,301,875	15	220,125	6.21	6	8.70	9
HI	429,013	4	107,253	2.16	2	1.81	2
ID	598,447	4	149,612	1.21	1	2.74	3
IL	5,274,322	21	251,158	11.51	12	9.34	9
IN	2,468,002	11	224,364	4.32	4	6.59	7
IA	1,506,908	7	215,273	3.45	3	3.49	4
KS	1,187,756	6	197,959	2.20	2	3.72	4
KY	1,795,860	8	224,483	3.18	3	4.76	5
LA	1,943,106	9	215,901	3.80	4	5.10	5
ME	740,752	4	185,188	2.14	2	1.78	2
MD	2,386,678	10	238,668	5.59	6	4.29	4
MA	2,912,388	12	242,699	7.43	8	4.41	4
MI	4,839,252	17	284,662	8.71	9	8.13	8
MN	2,828,387	10	282,839	5.11	5	4.76	5
MS	1,152,365	6	192,061	2.39	2	3.57	4
MO	2,731,364	11	248,306	5.07	5	5.86	6
MT	450,445	3	150,148	1.16	1	1.77	2
NE	778,186	5	155,637	1.63	2	3.29	3
NV	829,587	5	165,917	2.39	2	2.52	3
NH	677,738	4	169,435	2.01	2	1.95	2
NJ	3,611,691	15	240,779	7.94	8	6.94	7
NM	756,304	5	151,261	2.45	2	2.49	3
NY	7,391,036	31	238,421	18.10	19	12.43	12
NC	3,501,007	15	233,400	6.54	7	8.40	8
ND	312,833	3	104,278	1.06	1	1.89	2
OH	5,627,908	20	281,395	9.74	10	10.16	10
OK	1,463,758	7	209,108	2.41	2	4.59	5
OR	1,836,782	7	262,397	3.59	4	3.30	3
PA	5,769,590	21	274,742	10.69	11	10.17	10
RI	437,134	4	109,284	2.38	2	1.55	2
SC	1,617,730	8	202,216	3.27	3	4.64	5
SD	388,215	3	129,405	1.15	1	1.80	2
TN	2,437,319	11	221,574	4.68	5	6.25	6
TX	7,410,765	34	217,964	13.00	13	20.77	21
UT	927,844	5	185,569	1.30	1	3.58	4
VT	312,309	3	104,103	1.77	2	1.16	1
VA	3,198,367	13	246,028	5.91	6	6.98	7
WA	2,859,084	11	259,917	5.81	6	5.02	5
WV	755,887	5	151,177	2.16	2	2.80	3
WI	2,997,007	10	299,701	4.97	5	4.93	5
WY	243,428	3	81,143	0.87	1	2.07	2
Totals		538		258	260	275	278
			Popular Vote Percentage	48.27%		50.73%	
			Equal Voice Vote Percentage	48.33%		51.67%	

2000 Presidential Election

Look at the map: The map below shows that 20 states were awarded to Gore and Bush won the remaining 30. It would appear that the country overwhelmingly voted for Bush. However, Gore actually won the popular vote. Bush still edged him out of the race by only four electoral votes! This is the only race of the nine examples wherein the winning candidate lost the popular vote.

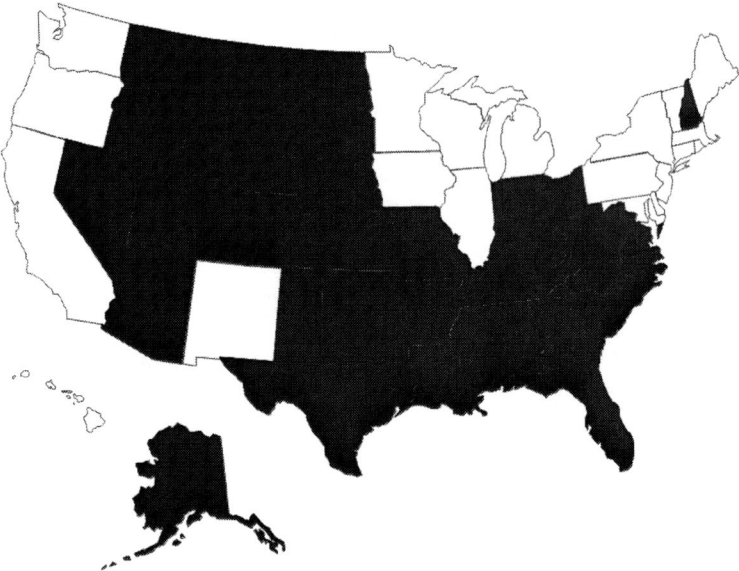

Figure 67: 2000 Electoral Vote Map

Things to consider: The race becomes even closer using the EV method because Gore would have won by only one vote! The data shows that a small increase in voter turn-out for Bush in New Mexico would have flipped the results in his favor. Gore won the deciding vote in New Mexico because of the adjustment rule for too few EVVs accrued for the state. Gore won 286,783 popular votes to Bush's

286,417. One vote had to be added, as per the adjustment rule, so it would have been awarded to Gore. Nader won 21,251 votes. The race shows that winning the popular vote generally carries the day. There were 12 states that tied in the number of Equal Voice Votes (EVVs).

Using the current Electoral College method, Connecticut, Hawaii, Massachusetts, New Hampshire, Rhode Island, and Vermont experienced having every county being carried by only one party. Using the EV voting method, the voting voice of those states are split by the following percentages showing many votes in these states were not represented:

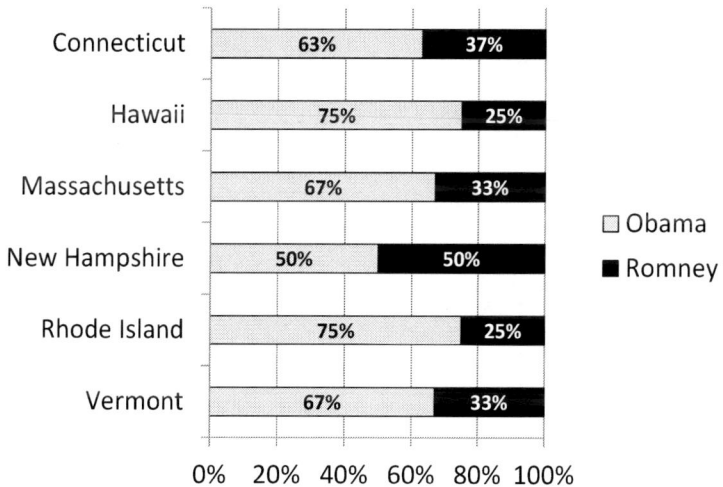

Figure 68: 2000 Selected State Voting Graph

Seven states (highlighted in gray in the next table) tied in the number of EVVs. Only Washington D.C. (highlighted in black in the next table) awarded all of its EVVs to one candidate.

Table 15: 2000 Example Election Results

States	Popular Vote	Electoral Votes	PVV	Gore	Gore EVVs	Bush	Bush EVVs	Nader	Nader EVVs
AL	1,661,953	9	184,661	3.79	4	5.11	5	0.10	0
AK	220,867	3	73,622	0.86	1	1.83	2	0.31	0
AZ	1,323,895	8	165,487	3.69	4	4.07	4	0.24	0
AR	901,072	6	150,179	2.78	3	3.13	3	0.09	0
CA	9,681,799	54	179,293	29.31	29	22.62	23	2.08	2
CO	1,686,976	8	210,872	3.44	3	4.13	5	0.43	0
CT	1,394,186	8	174,273	4.53	5	3.13	3	0.34	0
DE	326,007	3	108,669	1.66	2	1.26	1	0.08	0
DC	188,949	3	62,983	2.57	3	0.27	0	0.16	0
FL	5,922,531	25	236,901	12.29	12	12.30	13	0.41	0
GA	2,505,159	13	192,705	5.71	6	7.29	7	0.00	0
HI	364,603	4	91,151	2.25	2	1.51	2	0.24	0
ID	474,653	4	118,663	1.17	1	2.83	3	0.00	0
IL	4,681,671	22	212,803	12.06	13	9.46	9	0.48	0
IN	2,119,914	12	176,660	5.03	5	6.97	7	0.00	0
IA	1,290,583	7	184,369	3.44	4	3.41	3	0.15	0
KS	1,041,028	6	173,505	2.25	2	3.54	4	0.21	0
KY	1,530,589	8	191,324	3.33	3	4.55	5	0.12	0
LA	1,735,324	9	192,814	4.10	4	4.80	5	0.11	0
ME	637,211	4	159,303	1.98	2	1.78	2	0.24	0
MD	1,915,333	10	191,533	5.71	6	4.02	4	0.27	0
MA	2,660,039	12	221,670	7.26	8	3.95	4	0.78	0
MI	4,158,132	18	231,007	9.27	10	8.38	8	0.35	0
MN	2,404,862	10	240,486	4.86	5	4.62	5	0.53	0
MS	955,830	7	136,547	2.92	3	4.02	4	0.06	0
MO	2,338,835	11	212,621	5.22	5	5.59	6	0.18	0
MT	401,506	3	133,835	1.03	1	1.79	2	0.18	0
NE	647,310	5	129,462	1.67	2	3.16	3	0.18	0
NV	596,492	4	149,123	1.88	2	2.02	2	0.10	0
NH	561,144	4	140,286	1.90	2	1.95	2	0.16	0
NJ	3,069,145	15	204,610	8.45	9	6.10	6	0.45	0
NM	594,451	5	118,890	2.41	3	2.41	2	0.18	0
NY	6,182,796	33	187,357	19.97	20	11.84	12	1.19	1
NC	2,843,959	14	203,140	6.09	6	7.91	8	0.00	0
ND	280,794	3	93,598	1.02	1	1.88	2	0.10	0
OH	4,526,078	21	215,528	9.82	10	10.64	11	0.53	0
OK	1,218,661	8	152,333	3.11	3	4.89	5	0.00	0
OR	1,511,276	7	215,897	3.34	4	3.31	3	0.36	0
PA	4,832,174	23	210,095	11.73	12	10.78	11	0.49	0
RI	409,171	4	102,293	2.47	3	1.29	1	0.24	0
SC	1,403,977	8	175,497	3.29	3	4.59	5	0.12	0
SD	309,265	3	103,088	1.15	1	1.85	2	0.00	0
TN	2,053,963	11	186,724	5.24	5	5.66	6	0.11	0
TX	6,361,740	32	198,804	12.21	12	19.10	20	0.69	0
UT	749,554	5	149,911	1.35	1	3.42	4	0.24	0
VT	287,249	3	95,750	1.55	2	1.25	1	0.21	0
VA	2,702,740	13	207,903	5.85	6	6.86	7	0.28	0
WA	1,747,939	11	158,904	5.56	6	5.00	5	0.44	0
WV	631,236	5	126,247	2.31	2	2.61	3	0.08	0
WI	2,571,031	11	233,730	5.31	6	5.29	5	0.40	0
WY	208,095	3	69,365	0.87	1	2.13	2	0.00	0
Totals		538		261	268	262	267	16	3
			Popular Vote Percentage	48.77%		48.56%		2.67%	
			Equal Voice Vote Percentage	49.81%		49.63%		0.56%	

1996 Presidential Election

Look at the map: The 1996 presidential election shows
31 states were won by Clinton. Yet, he won the popular vote
by less than 9%! It's confusing, then, when one realizes
that Clinton won more than twice the electoral votes than
did Dole. Again, Ross Perot made a difference by capturing
over 8.5% of the popular vote, which was a significant
showing by a third-party candidate.

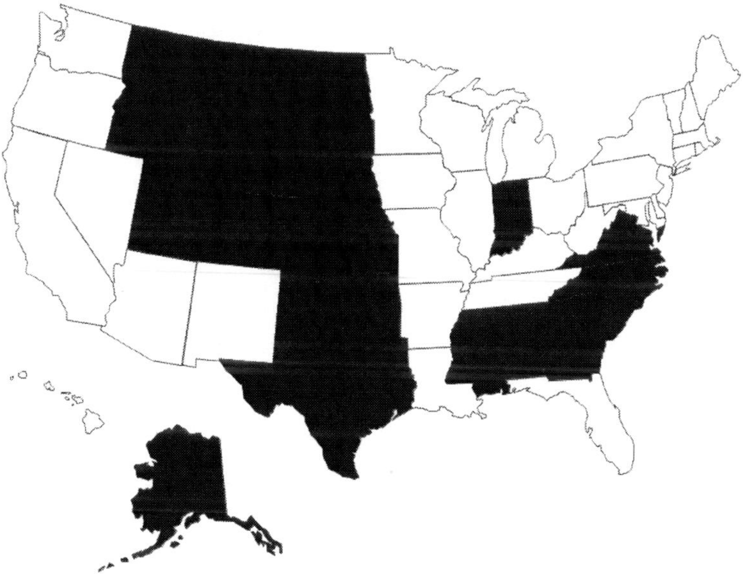

Figure 69: 1996 Electoral Vote Map

Things to consider: The 1996 presidential election
becomes very significant if the EV voting method was used.
Instead of enjoying a 41% margin of victory of electoral
votes, Clinton would have seen a much closer race with
only a 8.18% margin win. Even with the third-party
candidate showing well. The close race would be better
represented by the map shown above.

Equal Voice Voting

Using the current Electoral College method, Delaware, Hawaii, Maine, Massachusetts, Rhode Island, and Vermont experienced having every county being carried by only one party. Using the EV voting method, the voting voice of those states are split by the following percentages showing many votes in these states were not represented:

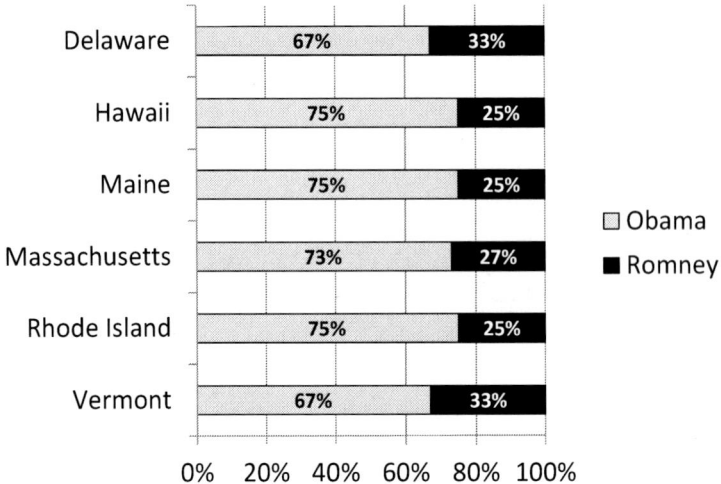

Figure 70: 1996 Selected State Voting Graph

Seven states (highlighted in gray in the next table) tied in the number of EVVs. Only Washington D.C. (highlighted in black in the next table) awarded all of its EVVs to one candidate.

Equal Voice Voting

Table 16: 1996 Example Election Results

States	Current Elect.	Electoral Votes	PVV	Clinton	Clinton EVVs	Dole	Dole EVVs	Perot	Perot EVVs
AL	1,523,358	9	169,262	3.91	4	4.54	5	0.54	0
AK	229,459	3	76,486	1.05	1	1.60	2	0.34	0
AZ	1,387,433	8	173,429	3.77	4	3.59	4	0.65	0
AR	870,471	6	145,079	3.28	4	2.24	2	0.48	0
CA	9,646,062	54	178,631	28.66	29	21.43	21	3.91	4
CO	1,462,629	8	182,829	3.67	4	3.78	4	0.54	0
CT	1,358,372	8	169,797	4.33	5	2.85	3	0.82	0
DE	268,136	3	89,379	1.57	2	1.11	1	0.32	0
DC	179,170	3	59,723	2.65	3	0.29	0	0.06	0
FL	5,273,068	25	210,923	12.07	12	10.64	11	2.29	2
GA	2,281,029	13	175,464	6.01	6	6.16	7	0.83	0
HI	346,313	4	86,578	2.37	3	1.32	1	0.32	0
ID	484,556	4	121,139	1.37	1	2.12	3	0.52	0
IL	4,275,173	22	194,326	12.05	12	8.17	8	1.78	2
IN	2,118,416	12	176,535	5.03	5	5.70	6	1.27	1
IA	1,218,061	7	174,009	3.56	4	2.83	3	0.60	0
KS	1,063,543	6	177,257	2.19	2	3.29	4	0.52	0
KY	1,380,293	8	172,537	3.69	4	3.61	4	0.70	0
LA	1,763,716	9	195,968	4.73	5	3.64	4	0.63	0
ME	585,136	4	146,284	2.14	3	1.27	1	0.59	0
MD	1,763,549	10	176,355	5.48	6	3.86	4	0.66	0
MA	2,516,773	12	209,731	7.49	8	3.42	3	1.08	1
MI	3,807,535	18	211,530	9.41	9	7.00	7	1.59	2
MN	2,144,618	10	214,462	5.22	5	3.57	4	1.20	1
MS	886,082	7	126,583	3.11	3	3.47	4	0.41	0
MO	2,133,139	11	193,922	5.29	5	4.59	5	1.12	1
MT	402,803	3	134,268	1.25	1	1.34	2	0.41	0
NE	671,506	5	134,301	1.76	2	2.71	3	0.53	0
NV	447,204	4	111,801	1.82	2	1.78	2	0.39	0
NH	491,039	4	122,760	2.01	2	1.60	2	0.39	0
NJ	3,017,594	15	201,173	8.21	9	5.48	5	1.30	1
NM	538,503	5	107,701	2.54	3	2.16	2	0.30	0
NY	6,193,127	33	187,671	20.01	20	10.30	10	2.68	3
NC	2,501,846	14	178,703	6.20	6	6.86	8	0.94	0
ND	264,470	3	88,157	1.21	1	1.42	2	0.37	0
OH	4,491,312	21	213,872	10.04	10	8.70	9	2.26	2
OK	1,201,208	8	150,151	3.25	3	3.88	5	0.87	0
OR	1,309,014	7	187,002	3.47	4	2.88	3	0.65	0
PA	4,447,972	23	193,390	11.46	12	9.31	9	2.23	2
RI	381,456	4	95,364	2.44	3	1.10	1	0.46	0
SC	1,144,127	8	143,016	3.54	4	4.01	4	0.45	0
SD	321,126	3	107,042	1.30	1	1.41	2	0.29	0
TN	1,878,594	11	170,781	5.32	6	5.06	5	0.62	0
TX	5,574,387	32	174,200	14.12	14	15.71	16	2.17	2
UT	650,005	5	130,001	1.70	2	2.78	3	0.51	0
VT	249,270	3	83,090	1.66	2	0.97	1	0.37	0
VA	2,389,271	13	183,790	5.94	6	6.19	7	0.87	0
WA	2,165,038	11	196,822	5.71	6	4.27	4	1.02	1
WV	633,397	5	126,679	2.59	3	1.85	2	0.57	0
WI	2,144,339	11	194,940	5.50	6	4.33	4	1.17	1
WY	209,250	3	69,750	1.12	1	1.51	2	0.37	0
Totals		538		268	278	224	234	46	26
Popular Vote Percentage				50.38%		42.07%		7.56%	
Equal Voice Vote Percentage				51.67%		43.49%		4.83%	

1992 Presidential Election

Look at the map: Bush won 18 states in 1992 and captured a little more than 37% of the popular vote. Perot won 19% of the popular vote, which means Clinton only won the popular vote by a 5.6% margin. Still, Clinton more than doubled the electoral votes won by Bush. This was the most significant third-party race run of the nine examples shown, with Perot winning over 19% of the popular vote.

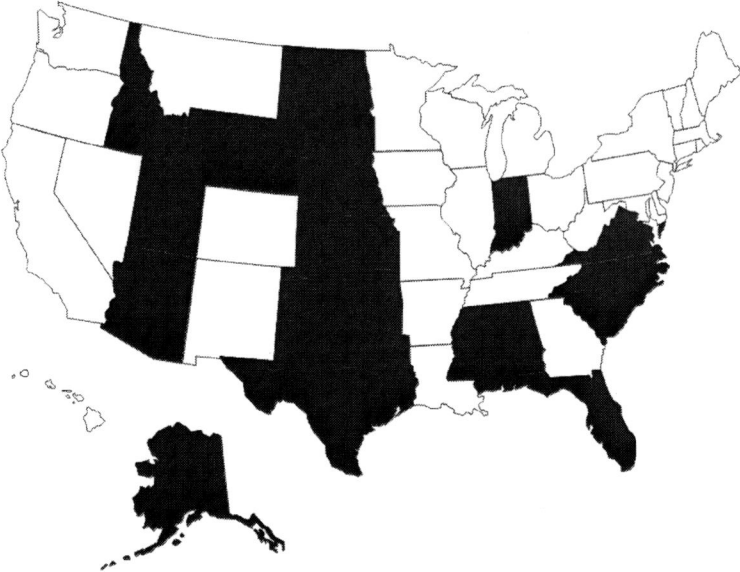

Figure 71: 1992 Electoral Vote Map

Things to consider: The 1992 electoral voting would have been much narrower if the EV voting method had been used. Instead of Clinton winning by a 2 to 1 margin, he would have realized only a 5.57% margin of victory. This race had the most states evenly splitting the EVVs than in any of the nine examples shown. It becomes even more significant when Ross Perot's share of the electoral votes would have been 15.6% of the EVVs!

Using the current Electoral College method, Hawaii, Maine, and Rhode Island experienced having every county being carried by only one party. Using the EV voting method, the voting voice of those states are split by the following percentages showing many votes in these states were not represented:

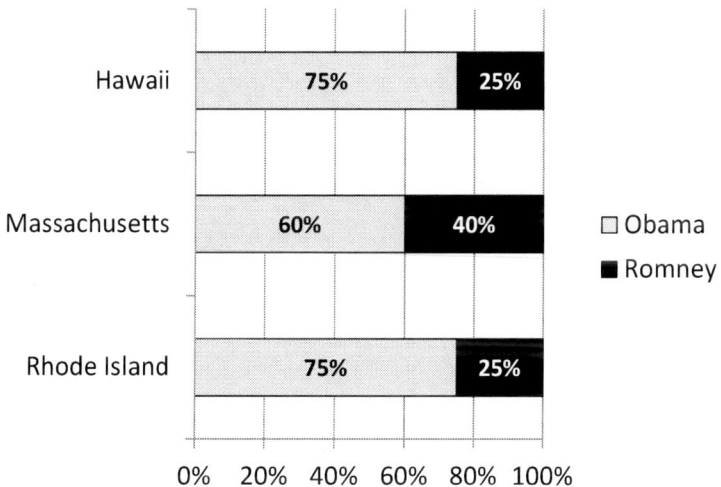

Figure 72: 1992 Selected State Voting Graph

Eleven states (highlighted in gray in the next table) tied in the number of EVVs. Three states and Washington D.C. (highlighted in black in the next table) awarded all of their EVVs to one candidate.

Equal Voice Voting

Table 17: 1992 Example Election Results

States	Popular Vote	Electoral Votes	PVV	Clinton	Clinton EVVs	Bush	Bush EVVs	Perot	Perot EVVs
AL	1,677,472	9	186,386	3.70	4	4.32	5	0.98	0
AK	253,775	3	84,592	0.93	0	1.21	3	0.87	0
AZ	1,468,877	8	183,610	2.96	3	3.12	3	1.93	2
AR	942,279	6	157,047	3.22	4	2.15	2	0.63	0
CA	11,047,905	54	204,591	25.03	25	17.75	18	11.22	11
CO	1,558,541	8	194,818	3.23	3	2.89	3	1.88	2
CT	1,609,402	8	201,175	3.39	3	2.87	3	1.73	2
DE	287,580	3	95,860	1.31	2	1.07	1	0.62	0
DC	222,998	3	74,333	2.59	3	0.28	0	0.13	0
FL	5,295,913	25	211,837	9.78	10	10.25	10	4.97	5
GA	2,313,875	13	177,990	5.67	6	5.59	5	1.74	1
HI	369,135	4	92,284	1.94	3	1.48	1	0.57	1
ID	470,053	4	117,513	1.17	1	1.72	2	1.11	1
IL	5,027,961	22	228,544	10.73	11	7.59	8	3.68	3
IN	2,293,729	12	191,144	4.44	4	5.18	6	2.39	2
IA	1,344,712	7	192,102	3.05	3	2.63	3	1.32	1
KS	1,152,743	6	192,124	2.03	2	2.34	2	1.63	2
KY	1,486,226	8	185,778	3.58	4	3.32	3	1.10	1
LA	1,760,835	9	195,648	4.17	4	3.75	4	1.08	1
ME	676,744	4	169,186	1.56	2	1.22	1	1.22	1
MD	1,977,079	10	197,708	5.00	5	3.58	4	1.42	1
MA	2,754,409	12	229,534	5.74	6	3.51	4	2.75	2
MI	4,250,935	18	236,163	7.92	8	6.58	7	3.49	3
MN	2,331,344	10	233,134	4.38	5	3.21	3	2.41	2
MS	973,677	7	139,097	2.88	3	3.51	4	0.62	0
MO	2,383,773	11	216,707	4.86	5	3.74	4	2.39	2
MT	405,939	3	135,313	1.14	2	1.07	1	0.79	0
NE	734,646	5	146,929	1.48	1	2.34	3	1.18	1
NV	497,556	4	124,389	1.52	2	1.41	1	1.07	1
NH	532,861	4	133,215	1.57	2	1.52	2	0.91	0
NJ	3,314,900	15	220,993	6.50	7	6.14	6	2.36	2
NM	566,336	5	113,267	2.31	3	1.88	2	0.81	0
NY	6,881,820	33	208,540	16.52	17	11.25	11	5.23	5
NC	2,603,567	14	185,969	5.99	6	6.09	6	1.92	2
ND	306,496	3	102,165	0.97	0	1.33	3	0.70	0
OH	4,915,678	21	234,080	8.48	9	8.09	8	4.43	4
OK	1,385,873	8	173,234	2.73	3	3.42	3	1.85	2
OR	1,451,162	7	207,309	3.00	3	2.29	2	1.71	2
PA	4,933,672	23	214,507	10.44	11	8.35	8	4.21	4
RI	449,945	4	112,486	1.90	3	1.17	1	0.93	0
SC	1,195,893	8	149,487	3.21	3	3.86	5	0.93	0
SD	334,901	3	111,634	1.12	1	1.22	2	0.66	0
TN	1,974,789	11	179,526	5.20	5	4.69	5	1.11	1
TX	6,132,667	32	191,646	11.91	12	13.02	13	7.07	7
UT	709,461	5	141,892	1.29	1	2.27	3	1.43	1
VT	287,697	3	95,899	1.39	3	0.92	0	0.69	0
VA	2,537,806	13	195,216	5.32	5	5.89	6	1.79	2
WA	2,266,051	11	206,005	4.82	5	3.55	4	2.63	2
WV	681,804	5	136,361	2.43	3	1.77	2	0.80	0
WI	2,516,400	11	228,764	4.55	5	4.07	4	2.38	2
WY	198,770	3	66,257	1.03	1	1.20	2	0.77	0
Totals		538	232		242	204	212	102	84
Popular Vote Percentage				43.29%		37.69%		19.03%	
Equal Voice Vote Percentage				44.98%		39.41%		15.61%	

Page E-16

1988 Presidential Election

Look at the map: Only 10 states were won by Dukakis in 1988. At first glance, that would seem to be 25% of the nation, yet Dukakis won over 46% of the popular vote. With such a voter turn-out in his favor, it's rather amazing he captured only 20.8% of the electoral votes. That story is not represented by the map shown here!

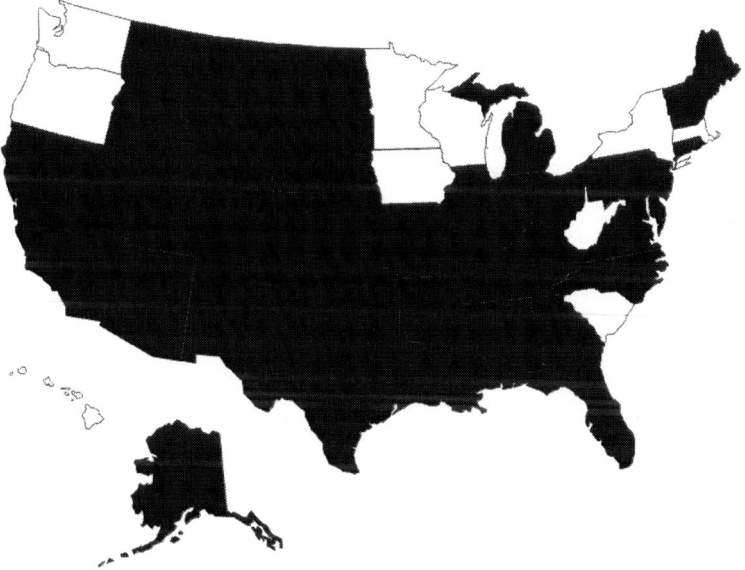

Figure 73: 1988 Electoral Vote Map

Things to consider: Instead of winning the election by more than a 58% margin in the electoral voting, the EV voting method would have reduced that margin to just a little more than 8%! It's obvious that a lot of Democratic voters were essentially disenfranchised in this election.

Using the current Electoral College method, Delaware, Nevada, Rhode Island, and Wyoming experienced having every county being carried by only one party. Using the EV voting method, the voting voice of those states are split by the following percentages showing many votes in these states were not represented:

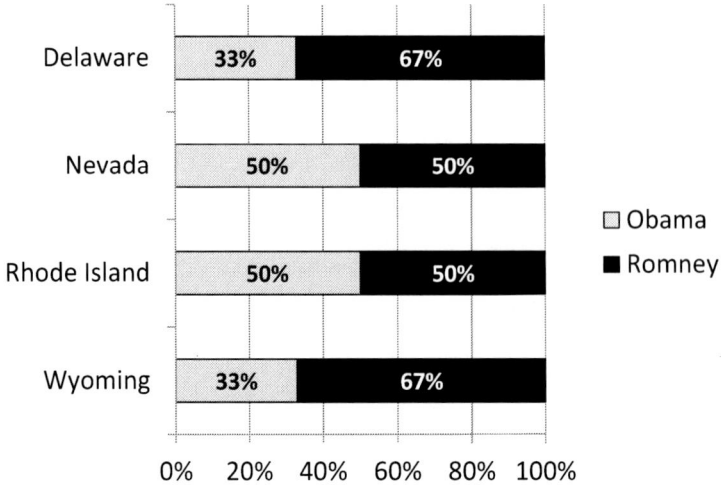

Figure 74: 1988 Selected State Voting Graph

Thirteen states (highlighted in gray in the next table) tied in the number of EVVs. Only Washington D.C. (highlighted in black in the next table) awarded all of its EVVs to one candidate.

Equal Voice Voting

Table 18: 1988 Example Election Results

States	Popular Vote	Electoral Votes	PVV	Dukakis	Dukakis EVVs	Bush	Bush EVVs
AL	1,365,082	9	151,676	3.62	4	5.38	5
AK	191,835	3	63,945	1.14	1	1.86	2
AZ	1,156,570	7	165,224	2.75	3	4.25	4
AR	815,815	6	135,969	2.57	3	3.43	3
CA	9,757,150	47	207,599	22.65	23	24.35	24
CO	1,349,630	8	168,704	3.68	4	4.32	4
CT	1,426,825	8	178,353	3.79	4	4.21	4
DE	248,286	3	82,762	1.31	1	1.69	2
DC	186,997	3	62,332	2.56	3	0.44	0
FL	4,272,448	21	203,450	8.14	8	12.86	13
GA	1,796,123	12	149,677	4.78	5	7.22	7
HI	350,989	4	87,747	2.19	2	1.81	2
ID	401,153	4	100,288	1.47	1	2.53	3
IL	4,526,879	24	188,620	11.75	12	12.25	12
IN	2,158,406	12	179,867	4.78	5	7.22	7
IA	1,215,912	8	151,989	4.41	4	3.59	4
KS	976,685	7	139,526	3.03	3	3.97	4
KY	1,314,649	9	146,072	3.97	4	5.03	5
LA	1,601,162	10	160,116	4.48	4	5.52	6
ME	550,700	4	137,675	1.77	2	2.23	2
MD	1,702,471	10	170,247	4.85	5	5.15	5
MA	2,596,050	13	199,696	7.02	7	5.98	6
MI	3,641,269	20	182,063	9.20	9	10.80	11
MN	2,071,808	10	207,181	5.36	5	4.64	5
MS	921,811	7	131,687	2.76	3	4.24	4
MO	2,086,572	11	189,688	5.28	5	5.72	6
MT	359,348	4	89,837	1.88	2	2.12	2
NE	657,191	5	131,438	1.97	2	3.03	3
NV	338,778	4	84,695	1.57	2	2.43	2
NH	445,233	4	111,308	1.47	1	2.53	3
NJ	3,058,145	16	191,134	6.89	7	9.11	9
NM	514,838	5	102,968	2.37	2	2.63	3
NY	6,429,753	36	178,604	18.74	19	17.26	17
NC	2,127,425	13	163,648	5.44	5	7.56	8
ND	294,298	3	98,099	1.30	1	1.70	2
OH	4,356,178	23	189,399	10.24	10	12.76	13
OK	1,161,790	8	145,224	3.33	3	4.67	5
OR	1,176,332	7	168,047	3.67	4	3.33	3
PA	4,495,031	25	179,801	12.21	12	12.79	13
RI	402,884	4	100,721	2.24	2	1.76	2
SC	976,997	8	122,125	3.03	3	4.97	5
SD	310,975	3	103,658	1.40	1	1.60	2
TN	1,627,027	11	147,912	4.60	5	6.40	6
TX	5,389,577	29	185,847	12.66	13	16.34	16
UT	635,794	5	127,159	1.63	2	3.37	3
VT	240,106	3	80,035	1.45	1	1.55	2
VA	2,168,961	12	180,747	4.76	5	7.24	7
WA	1,837,351	10	183,735	5.08	5	4.92	5
WV	651,081	6	108,514	3.14	3	2.86	3
WI	2,174,293	11	197,663	5.70	6	5.30	5
WY	173,980	3	57,993	1.16	1	1.84	2
Totals		538			247		291
					247		291
			Popular Vote Percentage		46.10%		53.90%
			Equal Voice Vote Percentage		45.91%		54.09%

1984 Presidential Election

Look at the map: The 1984 election was won by 97.6% (Reagan) of the electoral vote versus 2.4% (Mondale). Only Minnesota and Washington D.C. was won by Mondale. Still Mondale won 40.89% of the popular vote, which is not at all apparent when viewing the map below.

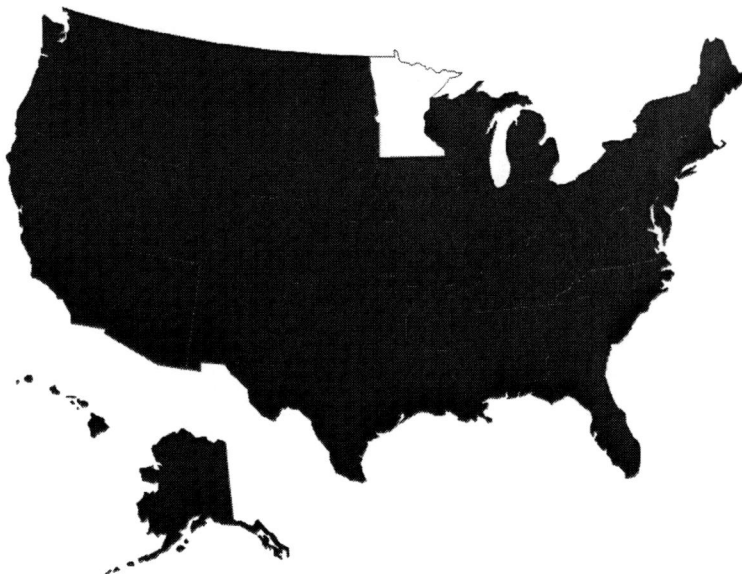

Figure 75: 1984 Electoral Vote Map

Things to consider: If the EV voting method had been used, the percentages would have been 59.48% (Reagan) versus 40.52% (Mondale). It still would have been a very decisive win, but not one that left much of the populace wondering how they were so poorly represented in the results.

Using the current Electoral College method, Alaska, Delaware, Hawaii, Idaho, Nebraska, Nevada, New Hampshire, Utah, and Wyoming experienced having every county being carried by only one party. Using the EV voting method, the voting voice of those states are split by the following percentages showing many votes in these states were not represented:

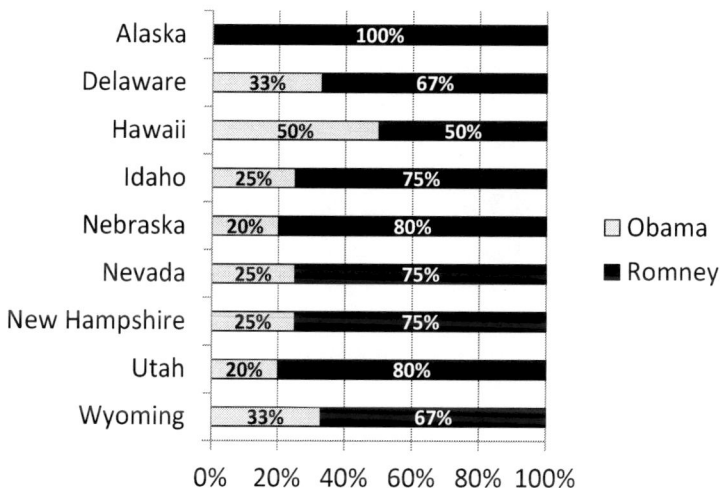

Figure 76: 1984 Selected State Voting Graph

Eight states (highlighted in gray in the next table) tied in the number of EVVs. One state and Washington D.C. (highlighted in black in the next table) awarded all of their EVVs to one candidate.

Table 19: 1984 Example Election Results

States	Popular Vote	Electoral Votes	PVV	Mondale	Mondale EVVs	Reagan	Reagan EVVs
AL	1,524,748	9	169,416	3.85	4	5.15	5
AK	200,384	3	66,795	0.93	0	2.07	3
AZ	1,015,270	7	145,039	2.30	2	4.70	5
AR	873,420	6	145,570	2.33	2	3.67	4
CA	9,121,357	47	194,071	19.66	20	27.34	27
CO	1,276,792	8	159,599	2.85	3	5.15	5
CT	1,460,474	8	182,559	3.12	3	4.88	5
DE	253,846	3	84,615	1.20	1	1.80	2
DC	209,417	3	69,806	2.58	3	0.42	0
FL	4,177,099	21	198,909	7.28	7	13.72	14
GA	1,775,350	12	147,946	4.78	5	7.22	7
HI	332,032	4	83,008	1.77	2	2.23	2
ID	406,033	4	101,508	1.07	1	2.93	3
IL	4,793,602	24	199,733	10.45	10	13.55	14
IN	2,218,711	12	184,893	4.55	5	7.45	7
IA	1,308,708	8	163,589	3.70	4	4.30	4
KS	1,007,117	7	143,874	2.31	2	4.69	5
KY	1,352,101	9	150,233	3.57	4	5.43	5
LA	1,688,885	10	168,889	3.86	4	6.14	6
ME	551,015	4	137,754	1.56	2	2.44	2
MD	1,667,853	10	166,785	4.72	5	5.28	5
MA	2,550,542	13	196,196	6.32	6	6.68	7
MI	3,781,209	20	189,060	8.09	8	11.91	12
MN	2,068,967	10	206,897	5.01	5	4.99	5
MS	934,569	7	133,510	2.64	3	4.36	4
MO	2,122,771	11	192,979	4.40	4	6.60	7
MT	379,192	4	94,798	1.55	2	2.45	2
NE	646,610	5	129,322	1.45	1	3.55	4
NV	280,425	4	70,106	1.31	1	2.69	3
NH	387,428	4	96,857	1.24	1	2.76	3
NJ	3,194,953	16	199,685	6.32	6	9.68	10
NM	508,870	5	101,774	1.98	2	3.02	3
NY	6,784,372	36	188,455	16.55	17	19.45	19
NC	2,170,768	13	166,982	4.94	5	8.06	8
ND	304,765	3	101,588	1.03	1	1.97	2
OH	4,503,999	23	195,826	9.32	9	13.68	14
OK	1,246,610	8	155,826	2.47	2	5.53	6
OR	1,222,179	7	174,597	3.07	3	3.93	4
PA	4,812,454	25	192,498	11.57	12	13.43	13
RI	409,186	4	102,297	1.93	2	2.07	2
SC	959,998	8	120,000	2.87	3	5.13	5
SD	316,380	3	105,460	1.10	1	1.90	2
TN	1,701,926	11	154,721	4.60	5	6.40	6
TX	5,382,704	29	185,610	10.50	11	18.50	18
UT	624,474	5	124,895	1.24	1	3.76	4
VT	231,595	3	77,198	1.24	1	1.76	2
VA	2,133,328	12	177,777	4.48	4	7.52	8
WA	1,850,022	10	185,002	4.32	4	5.68	6
WV	733,608	6	122,268	2.68	3	3.32	3
WI	2,194,324	11	199,484	4.99	5	6.01	6
WY	186,611	3	62,204	0.86	1	2.14	2
Totals		538			219		320
				218	319		
			Popular Vote Percentage	40.89%		59.11%	
			Equal Voice Vote Percentage	40.52%		59.48%	

1980 Presidential Election

Look at the map: 1980 showed the widest disparity, of the nine elections shown, between the electoral votes won by the Republicans versus the Democrats, winning an almost 9 to 1 ratio. Reagan captured 90.89% of the electoral votes while Carter only received 9.11%. The popular vote, on the other hand, shows Reagan won by less than 10%!

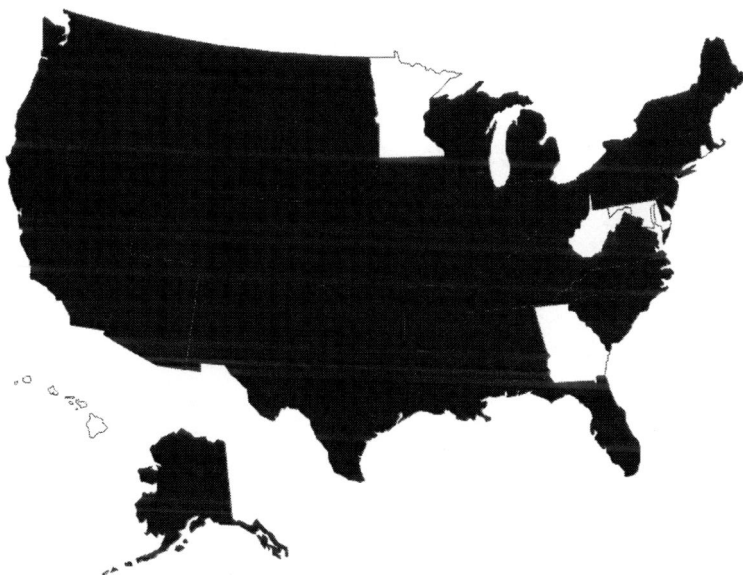

Figure 77: 1980 Electoral Vote Map

Things to consider: Using the EV voting method, Reagan's victory would have been by 77 EVVs, closer to a 14% margin instead of over 90%. This is a good example of how the current Electoral College can render an inaccurate picture of what truly has transpired across the country.

Using the current Electoral College method, Delaware, Nevada, Rhode Island, and Wyoming experienced having every county being carried by only one party. Using the EV voting method, the voting voice of those states are split by the following percentages showing many voter votes in these states were not represented:

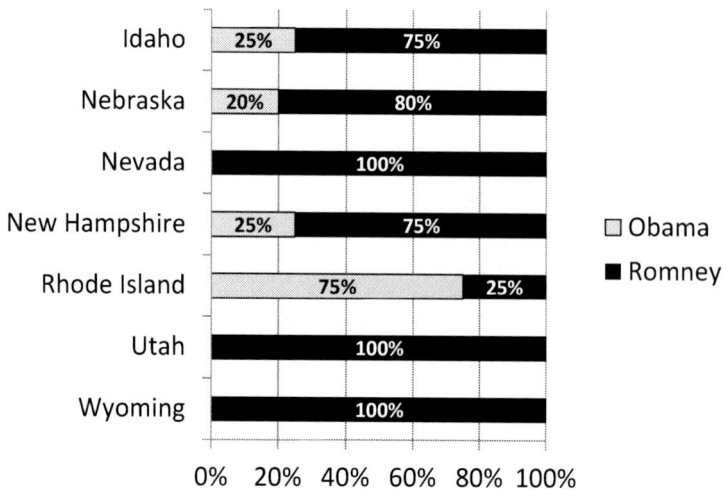

Figure 78: 1980 Selected State Voting Graph

Eight states (highlighted in gray in the next table) tied in the number of EVVs. Five states and Washington D.C. (highlighted in black in the next table) awarded all of their EVVs to one candidate.

Equal Voice Voting

Table 20: 1980 Example Election Results

States	Popular Vote	Electoral Votes	PVV	Carter	Carter EVVs	Reagan	Reagan EVVs	Anderson	Anderson EVVs
AL	1,307,403	9	145,267	4.38	4	4.50	5	0.11	0
AK	139,110	3	46,370	0.90	0	1.86	3	0.24	0
AZ	853,483	6	142,247	1.74	2	3.72	4	0.54	0
AR	823,673	6	137,279	2.90	3	2.94	3	0.16	0
CA	8,348,342	45	185,519	16.62	17	24.39	24	3.99	4
CO	1,150,870	7	164,410	2.24	2	3.97	5	0.79	0
CT	1,390,749	8	173,844	3.12	3	3.90	5	0.99	0
DE	233,294	3	77,765	1.36	1	1.43	2	0.21	0
DC	169,575	3	56,525	2.30	3	0.41	0	0.29	0
FL	3,656,118	17	215,066	6.60	7	9.52	10	0.88	0
GA	1,581,178	12	131,765	6.76	7	4.96	5	0.27	0
HI	298,012	4	74,503	1.82	2	1.75	2	0.43	0
ID	427,949	4	106,987	1.03	1	2.72	3	0.25	0
IL	4,686,216	26	180,239	10.99	11	13.08	13	1.92	2
IN	2,211,492	13	170,115	4.96	5	7.38	8	0.66	0
IA	1,300,331	8	162,541	3.13	3	4.16	5	0.71	0
KS	961,193	7	137,313	2.38	2	4.13	5	0.50	0
KY	1,282,818	9	142,535	4.32	4	4.46	5	0.22	0
LA	1,527,651	10	152,765	4.64	5	5.19	5	0.17	0
ME	512,823	4	128,206	1.72	2	1.86	2	0.42	0
MD	1,526,304	10	152,630	4.76	6	4.46	4	0.78	0
MA	2,496,393	14	178,314	5.93	6	5.92	6	2.15	2
MI	3,851,980	21	183,428	9.06	9	10.44	10	1.50	2
MN	2,002,438	10	200,244	4.77	6	4.36	4	0.87	0
MS	882,406	7	126,058	3.41	3	3.50	4	0.10	0
MO	2,083,283	12	173,607	5.36	5	6.19	7	0.45	0
MT	354,127	4	88,532	1.33	1	2.34	3	0.33	0
NE	630,492	5	126,098	1.32	1	3.32	4	0.36	0
NV	239,334	3	79,778	0.84	0	1.94	3	0.22	0
NH	380,262	4	95,066	1.15	1	2.33	3	0.52	0
NJ	2,928,553	17	172,268	6.66	7	8.98	9	1.36	1
NM	448,064	4	112,016	1.50	1	2.24	3	0.26	0
NY	6,090,004	41	148,537	18.37	18	19.48	20	3.15	3
NC	1,843,453	13	141,804	6.17	6	6.45	7	0.37	0
ND	296,444	3	98,815	0.80	0	1.96	3	0.24	0
OH	3,984,431	25	159,377	11.00	11	13.84	14	0.16	0
OK	1,135,880	8	141,985	2.83	3	4.90	5	0.27	0
OR	1,140,323	6	190,054	2.40	2	3.00	4	0.59	0
PA	4,488,533	27	166,242	11.63	12	13.61	14	1.76	1
RI	412,954	4	103,239	1.92	3	1.50	1	0.58	0
SC	881,365	8	110,171	3.89	4	3.99	4	0.13	0
SD	323,629	4	80,907	1.28	1	2.45	3	0.26	0
TN	1,606,803	10	160,680	4.87	5	4.90	5	0.22	0
TX	4,503,465	26	173,210	10.86	11	14.50	15	0.64	0
UT	594,237	4	148,559	0.84	0	2.96	4	0.20	0
VT	208,280	3	69,427	1.18	1	1.36	2	0.46	0
VA	1,837,201	12	153,100	4.91	5	6.46	7	0.62	0
WA	1,700,510	9	188,946	3.44	3	4.58	6	0.98	0
WV	733,359	6	122,227	3.01	3	2.73	3	0.26	0
WI	2,231,086	11	202,826	4.84	5	5.37	6	0.79	0
WY	172,199	3	57,400	0.86	0	1.93	3	0.21	0
Totals		538		225	223	278	300	35	15
			Popular Vote Percentage	41.81%		51.73%		6.47%	
			Equal Voice Vote Percentage	41.45%		55.76%		2.79%	

Equal Voice Voting

APPENDIX F – RESOURCES

Getty Images (2013, January 30) Clipart.com 10 Million Downloadable Images by Subscription! Archived at http://clipart.com

Leip, David (2012, December 15, and 2013, January 15) Atlas of U.S. Presidential Elections. Presidential Election Results for years 1980 through 2012, archived at http://uselectionatlas.org/results/index.html Note: Tables and data to derive graph results throughout this book were retrieved from this website.

NationalAtlas.gov. (2013, January 15). Printable Maps, archived at http://www.nationalatlas.gov/printable/ congress.html

United States House of Representatives. (2013, January 15). Find Your Representative, archived at http://www.house.gov/

United States Senate. (2013, January 15). Senators of the 113th Congress, archived at http://www.senate.gov/general/contact_information/s enators_cfm.cfm

Wikipedia, the free encyclopedia. (2013, January 15). Gerrymandering, archived at http://en.wikipedia.org/wiki/Gerrymandering

Wikipedia, the free encyclopedia. (2012, December 15). List of U.S. States by population density, archived at http://en.wikipedia.org/wiki/List_of_U.S._states_by_ population_density

About the Author

Jerry Spriggs grew up on a farm in North Dakota and has since lived in California, Arizona, and Oregon. Jerry is currently living in the Portland area with his wife, Jane. He has spent his career as an instructional designer, designing and developing training materials. It's a career which actually arose from his hobby of designing and developing board games covering such subjects as sports, ecology, financial, military, and children's interests. Jerry's work has spanned aeronautical, financial, automotive, educational, and technological industries.

Equal Voice Voting